# WHY MEN
# MARRY

## 150 Guys Reveal What Prompted Them to Pop the Question

### RUSSELL WILD

CONTEMPORARY BOOKS

**Library of Congress Cataloging-in-Publication Data**

Wild, Russell.
    Why men marry : 150 guys reveal what prompted them to pop the
question / Russell Wild.
        p.    cm.
    ISBN 0-8092-2978-1
    1. Marriage—United States.    2. Mate selection—United States.
3. Men—United States—Attitudes.    I. Title.
HQ734.W65    1998
306.81—dc21                                                      98-16842
                                                                     CIP

Cover design by Mary Lockwood
Interior design by Susan H. Hartman

Published by Contemporary Books
A division of NTC/Contemporary Publishing Group, Inc.
4255 West Touhy Avenue, Lincolnwood (Chicago), Illinois 60646-1975 U.S.A.
Printed in the United States of America
International Standard Book Number: 0-8092-2978-1
98  99  00  01  02  03  04  QP  16  15  14  13  12  11  10  9  8  7  6  5  4  3  2  1

# CONTENTS

Men don't need ultimatums . . . perhaps ■ Men marry
their best friends ■ But they tend to marry only good-

looking friends ■ Men love their college blind dates ■ Dinner and movie are top first-date spots ■ Diamonds look best under candlelight ■ We meet our dream woman first, then ponder marriage ■ Love is a familiar face ■ Love is quick—and, yes, absence *does* make the heart grow fonder ■ Forget the mother-in-law jokes ■ The "Rules" are ridiculous . . . maybe ■ Men get what they expect

Driven by chemistry ■ The need to belong ■ Deep psychology ■ Following religious dictates ■ Bending to her whim

Where the single men are

## PART TWO
# *Husband Talk*

## Notice

Some men are turned on by a keen mind and a warm soul. Other men go gaga for tight buns and great big orbs. Not all guys are anxious to go on record about their particular turn-ons. So, in the interest of encouraging total openness and honesty, only first names appear in this book. In a few cases, where the men were especially eager to cloak their identities, first names were changed. Beyond that, there is no fiction in this book. All the stories you'll read are real, as told in the men's own voices.

# ACKNOWLEDGMENTS

This entire book is a tribute to the ongoing relationship. So it seems apt that I begin the book by tipping my hat to a few ongoing relationships of my own. . . .

I am grateful to all the men who agreed to be interviewed for *Why Men Marry*. Some of these guys I've known for only a short while; with others I go way back. (Hey, Bobby! Hey, Dad!) I'm also grateful to the experts I interviewed, several of whom I've tapped for various magazine stories over the years: Kenneth Ferguson, Helen Fisher, Robert Gordon, John Gray, Robert Jaffe, Ray Klein, Yechezkel Kornfeld, Sarah Ossey, Riki

Robbins, Peter Sheras, Phyllis Koch-Sheras, Jim Sniechowski, and Maria Tjeltveit. Thanks also to Donna Miller and Dave Bradley of Matchmaker International.

Thanks, too, to Mary Ann Cavlin, my editor at *Modern Bride* (where I wrote my first article about marriage). Many thanks to Kara Leverte and all the others at Contemporary Books—this is our second project together, and both have been good experiences. Thanks also to Ellen Greene—this is the third book she's deftly agented for me. And thanks to Linda Dailey Paulson, who, from behind her computer in Sacramento, has helped me with research on this project and many others.

Finally, thank you, the Honorable Thomas Kuhl, formerly and perhaps still of Baltimore, for your sonorous rendition of Shakespeare's sonnets on July 4, 1981, my and Susan's wedding day. It was one of the best days of my life.

INTRODUCTION

# The Mystery of Matrimony

**M**ore than 90 percent of all men marry. Of those who lose or leave their wives, 80 percent marry again. What is it about the institution of marriage that men can't seem to resist? What calls and recalls more men to the altar than to the Super Bowl and the World Series combined?

My search for answers began with an article I wrote some time back for *Modern Bride* magazine. I found very little had ever been written on why men marry. But, at the same time, I discovered that nearly everyone I talked with (and especially single women) was very much curious. I started to wonder myself. I

knew, or thought I knew, why *I* married (which I suppose I'll have to reveal in Chapter 1). But how about all
those *other* guys, including several I knew from high
school and college, who swore they'd sooner join
monasteries than marry?

So. I interviewed eighty married and engaged men
from all walks of life—a U.S. Marine Corps sergeant, a
retired high official in the U.S. State Department, a
young warehouse worker, a trial lawyer, a college professor, a gynecologist, a circus clown. I sent out and
received back detailed questionnaires from another
seventy men—from Portland, Oregon, to Miami,
Florida, and from Paris, France, to Perth, Australia.
They ranged in age from nineteen to eighty-six. They
were white, black, Asian, and Hispanic. They were
first-time grooms and men married two, three—or in
the case of Thomas—*seven* times.

In addition to my own survey, I was given access to
information from the computer database of Matchmaker International of Pennsylvania, giving me valu-
able insights into the tastes and desires of an additional
1,100 single men on the make. Then I talked to the
experts—psychologists, relationships counselors, an
anthropologist, a minister, a rabbi, and a priest—and
got them to share their thoughts.

The job was lots of work but a lot of fun. No two husbands' stories were the same, and many of the responses I got were quite surprising. As you'll soon see for yourself . . .

Russell Wild

Rwild@Compuserve.com

# PART ONE

## The Marrying Man

# 1

# REVELATIONS AND CONFESSIONS

## What 150 Guys (and One Married Author) Have to Say

I remember the exact moment that I first saw marriage in my stars: I was eighteen. It was the summer after my freshman year of college. My buddies Bob (today a business executive in southern California), Lenny (now a scuba instructor somewhere in Florida, I believe), and I jumped into my gold 1969 Chevy Nova and drove out to the end of Long Island for a weekend of barhopping and beach volleyball. This was the infamous *Saturday Night Fever*/disco era, and we visited this one bar crawling with middle-aged, balding men in white suits and silk shirts open to the navel. Taking themselves for John Travolta, bobbing their heads to the music of the Bee Gees, they made repeated feeble attempts to woo the much younger women at the bar.

"My God," I said to myself, nursing my Harvey Wallbanger; "If that's what single life is like, it isn't for me."

In April of the next year, I met Susan at a college party. We dated, split up, dated some more. (I had decided to marry, yeah, but not at age nineteen! Not so soon!) After college, I ran off to work and play abroad (including six months in bachelor paradise, working as a yoga instructor for Club Med in Morocco), while Susan stayed in Washington, D.C., to start law school. Two years later, I returned briefly to Washington. She and I had a steamy reunion that lasted for about a week, after which I left for grad school in Arizona.

We traveled back and forth, spoke on the telephone, and she took off a summer to come join me in blistering Phoenix. (If that's not love, what is?) I took off a semester to spend time with her in D.C. Then, sometime in early November, during an evening phone call, she gave me an ultimatum. (To this day, Susan adamantly denies this ever happened!) She told me that she was having doubts about being able to continue with the relationship without a firm commitment from me. (Just the truth—no ultimatum, she swears.) I moped around for a couple of days, thinking how much happier I was when I was in her arms, how much we laughed together, and how much I loved her and her big, slobbering dog, Coco. And I thought of John Travolta.

I decided I would ask her to marry me.

On Thanksgiving break, I took her back to the location of the party where we had met in Washington five and one-half years earlier, and there, on the sidewalk at dusk, I asked for her hand. She said, "Yes." (I wasn't shocked.) We were married seven months later. That was seventeen years, several cities, two dogs and two cats, a few careers, and two childbirths ago.

And all this time, I thought that all men were just like me, wanting to marry, sort of, maybe, *someday* . . . but ultimately needing a woman to, well, push them before making the "big move." I was right in some cases, wrong in most. All of the men I surveyed were asked whether they ever got an ultimatum, and only a minority said they did. We'll call that . . .

# Revelation 1
## Men don't need ultimatums . . . perhaps

Fewer than 10 percent of all the men surveyed said they, like me, had received an ultimatum. According to Allan B., of Florida, for instance, "Christine said forget it—either we get married after graduation or she was moving on."

But does this mean that 90 percent of men jump into marriage without any kind of push on their beloved's part? No, I don't think so. I tend to suspect that many ultimatums are subtle and that many men wouldn't recognize an ultimatum if it slapped them between the eyes. (See Chapter 2, pages 26–27, for what relationships experts Riki Robbins, Ph.D., and Robert Jaffe, Ph.D., have to say on the subject.)

Now for eleven other revelations and confessions about why, how, and at what point men typically decide to marry; how they pick a mate; how they court; and how they propose.

# REVELATION 2

## Men marry their best friends

Three men in the survey mentioned the movie *When Harry Met Sally* . . . as really hitting home. No coincidence. Asked for the reasons they married, two-thirds of the guys mentioned "friendship/companionship"—the number one answer by far. This was followed by "children" (32 percent), "it was just the thing to do" (16 percent), and "to avoid dating" (16 percent). Other mentions: "gain respectability/social acceptability" (15 percent), "personal growth" (14 percent), "escape loneliness" (12 percent), "sex and romance" (12 percent), "cooking/housekeeping" (8 percent), "she gave me an ultimatum" (8 percent), and "fear of growing old/dying alone" (6 percent).

A handful of men say they used marriage as an excuse to flee their parents. Says Paul, fifty, a Pennsylvania business owner, "I was twenty-two, just home from my stint in Vietnam, back living with Mom and Dad, and not feeling too happy about it. Diane (who I met in night school) already had a house of her own. I saw her as my ticket to freedom."

Then there were the more unusual answers: Tim, a forty-one-year-old newspaper feature writer, found a lover and a friend in Elaine, but the real reason they married in 1988, he says, "was because of health insurance." He had it; she didn't.

# REVELATION 3
## But they tend to marry only good-looking friends

When asked "What did you initially find attractive about her?" 90 percent of the men mentioned some aspect of physical, above-the-neck attractiveness: "great eyes," "nice smile," or "long, blond hair." Forty-two percent brought up positive below-the-neck features, such as "nice legs," "firm butt," or "great breasts." In all, fewer than 5 percent of the men mentioned no physical characteristic whatsoever. The second most popular category, after looks, was "intelligence/education," mentioned by 59 percent of the men. That was followed by "common interests" (33 percent), "funny" (27 percent), and "happy" (27 percent).

Other mentionables:

- "Kind/nurturing" (25 percent)
- "Honest/loyal" (22 percent)
- "Easy to talk to" (15 percent)
- "Seemed like she'd be a good mom" (13 percent)
- "Financially responsible" (9 percent)
- "Spiritual" (8 percent)
- "Creative/artistic" (7 percent)
- "Great cook" (7 percent)
- "Innocent/pure" (5 percent)

# REVELATION 4

### Men love their college blind dates

Where do men meet their future brides? Twenty-four percent of all the men said "in college." Considering that far from all the guys in the survey even attended college, this percentage tells us that the halls of ivy are very fertile grounds for spouse hunting. Nearly the same percentage of men (22 percent) said that they met their wives on a blind date. Tied for third and fourth place, with 18 percent each, were "at work" and "at a party." Other ways that men meet their wives: "outing with mutual friends" (16 percent), "we knew each other as kids" (8 percent), "in high school or junior high" (8 percent), "at a bar" (6 percent), and "on-line/chat room" (6 percent).

And some less-common ways: "at a play," "on the street," "at the ice-skating rink," and "in the parking lot of our apartment building . . . She took out her tool kit and got my car started."

# Revelation 5

## Dinner and movie are top first-date spots

When husbands think back to that first date, 60 percent recall dinner at a restaurant. The second favorite activity for first dates is going to the movies (45 percent), which often follows dinner. Other favorite first-date ventures:

- ■ "Out for a drink"—alcohol or coffee
  (24 percent)

- "Sporting event" (14 percent)
- "Party" (12 percent)
- "Walk" (7 percent)
- "Dancing" (6 percent)
- "Concert" (5 percent)

# REVELATION 6

## Diamonds look best under candlelight

Where would the institution of marriage be if there were no classy restaurants? They are apparently men's favorite place to pop the big question. Of guys asked in our survey, nearly one-third presented the ring over a restaurant meal. Many guys (20 percent) do it while away with their gals on vacation. Another 20 percent popped the question in the comfort of home (most often a home both he and she shared). Eight percent asked "at the beach." Six percent asked "at a party or other public gathering." And another 6 percent said, "I can't remember."

Other answers included "at a cousin's wedding," "on top of a mountain," "in the back of a horse-drawn carriage," "riding on a train," and "on a roller coaster."

In 15 percent of the cases, it wasn't the man who popped the question, but the woman. Tom S. was asked by his girlfriend at a Dallas Cowboys football game. "At some point during the game, we had become extremely bored, and she looked over and asked me to marry her," he says.

And in 8 percent of the cases, the man "just assumed" that he and his girlfriend were going to marry—until, in about half of those situations (in the words of Midwest attorney Bruce), "Ariel made me get down on one knee and formally propose."

# Revelation 7

## We meet our dream woman first, then ponder marriage

The majority of men (55 percent) said they hadn't decided to marry until they met their future wives. "Marriage was the furthest thing from my mind!" says thirty-something Gene. In contrast, 40 percent said they had decided to marry before they met their true loves. "I always knew I'd find love, get married, and have two children," says Washington diplomat Pavel. The remaining 5 percent said, "I'm not sure" or "I can't remember."

# REVELATION 8

## Love is a familiar face

Asked if their brides reminded them of anyone, about half had someone in mind. Of those . . .

Thirty-seven percent named a showbiz or sports celebrity: "Sally Field," "Liz Taylor," "Gabriela Sabatini," "Joanie from 'Happy Days.'" Slightly less (35 percent) saw a resemblance to either "a former girlfriend" or "every girlfriend I've ever had." Eighteen percent saw something in their future wives that reminded them of mom (although Chris responded, "Thank God she didn't remind me of my mother! Thank God! Thank God!").

Other resemblances mentioned: "Grandma," "an aunt," "Venus," "my tenth-grade Spanish teacher," and "myself."

# REVELATION 9

## Love is quick—and, yes, absence *does* make the heart grow fonder

Asked when they first knew that *she* was the one, the men surveyed said

- ■ "Within the first several months to a year" (42 percent)

- "The first time we were apart" (22 percent)
- "The very moment I first saw her"
  (13 percent)
- "After our first night together" (12 percent)
- "After more than a year/several years"
  (12 percent)*
- "The first time we kissed" (8 percent)

Other answers: "even before we met (after communicating on-line)," "the first time I heard her sing," and "after we first made love . . . as soon as I caught my breath."

# REVELATION 10

## Forget the mother-in-law jokes

Despite the common quips about mothers-in-law from hell, nearly one in ten men said that the relationship with his wife's family was one of the things he relished about being married. "I love being a member of another family," says Richard, a thirty-six-year-old freelance writer. "This is something that gets short

---

* These slow-moving men tended to be teens when they met their future brides. Says Mike, who met Jessica in tenth grade, "I couldn't even contemplate marriage at that age, so I guess that no one would have qualified as 'the one.'"

shrift in all the mother-in-law jokes—the assumption always seems to be that in-laws are a pain, and that can certainly be true. That's true of any member of any family. Which to me is the whole point. No matter how much of a pain they are to you—or you are to them—you are intractably connected, and you have to deal with them."

A handful of men went so far as to say that the relationship they had with their prospective in-laws was actually one of the things that lulled them into marriage in the first place. "I was already thinking marriage, but what really made up my mind was meeting Audrey's family," says U.S. Marine Corps sergeant Jeremiah.

Of course, there are some men for whom in-law jokes are all too real: "I am still (after twenty years of marriage) wearing garlic around my neck whenever I visit them," says forty-two-year-old West Coast business exec Bob.

# REVELATION 11
## The "Rules" are ridiculous . . . maybe

Men may truly be attracted to women who play hard to get (as some bestselling authors have claimed), but the vast majority of men don't see it that way. Only 10 percent of those men I surveyed acknowledged that their wives had played hard to get. In fact, many men went out of their way to say that they were turned on by their girlfriends' *not* playing anything but rather by their complete candor.

"What made me marry her? Her straightforward-ness and openness—what you see is what you get," says California businessman David of his wife, Elizabeth.

It is possible that, just as in the case of the ultima-tums, women play hard to get in such subtle ways that men don't even notice them playing. Several responses I got sounded a bit fishy: "Play hard to get? No. When we were friends she was physically attracted to some-one else. It wasn't like she was playing hard to get—she just wasn't available," says scientist Tom, thirty-nine, of Wisconsin, speaking of his wife, Lisa.

Hmmmm.

# REVELATION 12
## Men get what they expect

We've all heard the glum statistics—half of all mar-riages end up in divorce. At any point in time, however, most marriages are happy ones. The Gallup Poll asked married men whether they would marry their wives all over again—93 percent said yes. Understandably. My survey found that the majority of men report getting what they wished for in marriage.

As you'll recall, two-thirds of men mentioned "friendship" among their top reasons for marrying. When asked what they loved about *being* married, three-quarters of married men said "friendship" or "companionship." In second place was "children," at 42 percent. Around one-third said either "dual income" or "sharing household responsibilities." And 15 percent said "having someone to grow old with."

Other things men love about their marriages: "sex" (12 percent), "home-cooked meals" (10 percent), and "her family" (10 percent). Many older men mentioned grandchildren. And some younger guys brought up "no longer feeling weird about being single," "not having people think I'm gay," "cheaper auto insurance," "always having a date for a movie," and "clean socks."

# 2

# THE SUBCONSCIOUS SIDE OF MARRIAGE

*Insights from the Experts*

As illuminating as this survey was, there is obviously a lot more to why men marry, and whom they choose to marry, than what they acknowledge. So much of what guys look for in marriage and a mate is difficult for them to articulate and very often subconscious, unconscious, or perhaps even instinctual.

One obvious example: not a single man surveyed said that he was attracted to his future wife for her youth (although some dropped in conversation that their wives were a decade or two younger). It doesn't take a lot of looking around to see that most men choose younger brides. The average American first-time groom marries a woman three years his junior. A man who marries a second time typically winds up with a wife five years younger. Obviously, men find youth desirable.

Such a premium on youth is part of what leads some researchers to conclude that men marry in response to evolutionary drives to procreate. They pick their wives partially based on subconscious cues that tell them whether she can bear children and raise them.

One proponent of this theory is social psychologist David M. Buss, Ph.D. In his book *The Evolution of Desire* (Basic Books, 1994), he writes:

> Ancestral men evolved mechanisms to sense cues to a woman's underlying reproductive value. These cues involve observable features of females. Two obvious cues are youth and health. Old or unhealthy women clearly could not reproduce as much as young, healthy women. Ancestral men solved the problem of finding reproductively valuable women in part by preferring those who are young and healthy.

Only one man in our survey mentioned his beloved's complexion, and no man said anything about his wife's wonderfully symmetrical face. Yet studies have shown that the more clear-skinned and symmetrical a woman's face, the more suitors she is likely to have. Buss and others would argue that those

are signs of good health, which men instinctually recognize as an indication of a woman's ability to bear
children.

Adequate-sized hips are also a sign of reproductive
fitness. Perhaps it's not surprising then that several
convincing analyses (of *Playboy* centerfold models and
other sexual epitomes) show that a woman with a hip-
to-waist ratio of 10:7 will be found most attractive by
the vast majority of men. (Although the centerfold models have gotten thinner over the years, their propor-
tions have remained surprisingly constant.)

Not one man in our survey specifically said he was
attracted to his wife for her "hip-to-waist ratio." But
there was certainly *plenty* of indication that men
notice, and seek out, good curvature.

## Driven by Chemistry

Some experts on male mating habits chalk up marriage, or a good part of marriage, to the activity of
powerful brain chemicals.

Although few guys surveyed said anything specifically about chemistry, suggestions were made that
chemistry was certainly involved. "I just flipped out
when I met her, and stayed flipped out for months
afterward. By the time I collected myself, I looked down
at my finger and it already had a ring on it!" says

Frank, of Baltimore, a thirty-four-year-old veterinarian and volunteer fund-raiser for the homeless.

"The brain is primed to fall in love and get manipulated. Chemicals, naturally occurring amphetamines that saturate the emotional centers of the brain, make you go out of your mind with love. You think that you want to spend the rest of your life with her, so you get married," says anthropologist Helen Fisher, Ph.D., author of *Anatomy of Love* (Fawcett Columbine, 1994). "How else could you explain that over 90 percent of Baby Boomers have married?" she asks. "Here's a generation that rejected all of its parents' values, yet they find marriage just as popular as did their parents."

Other chemicals, called *pheromones*, are known to dictate much coupling in the animal kingdom. To what extent the smell and taste of a woman guides men in their choice of a mate and their decision to marry remains open to speculation. A handful of men in our survey did mention smell, and although none specifically used the word *taste*, several did remark that there was something very, very special about their fiancées' kisses.

## The Need to Belong

Men, even cowboys and sailors, are not natural loners. We are a social species. We have a yearning to belong to a society and to be seen favorably by that society.

Marriage helps in this regard.

"Marriage gives legitimacy to a man. Married men in our society are seen as more reliable, stable, and beneficial to society," says Peter Sheras, Ph.D., clinical psychologist and marriage therapist at the University of Virginia. "Is this true? No, I don't think so. It's just the perception," he adds. "Say you first meet a guy named John, who is fifty-four years old, and has never been married. You'd probably assume that he is abnormal, weird, maybe gay. Most men wouldn't want others to think that."

Few men surveyed mentioned anything about legitimacy, so we have to conclude that most guys seek legitimacy from marriage on a mostly unconscious level.

One exception to this rule is Richard, a writer buddy of mine, who was most consciously out for legitimacy. "Before you get married, you're a kid, no matter how old you are. After you get married, you're a grown-up. I remember on our honeymoon gazing at my spouse and thinking to myself, 'I'm looking at my *wife*.' When we'd go shopping or out to a movie, my sense of myself was more mature and self-assured.

"More important," Richard continues, "I gained respect within my family. After I got married, my dad talked to me about stuff he never had before—like the nitty-gritty realities of providing for a family. He didn't have to tell me we were talking man-to-man. It was assumed. The same was true of my older married siblings, who treated me more as a peer. My younger brother, who is a never-married bachelor in his midthirties, has never been part of the club."

Peter Sheras's wife, Phyllis Koch-Sheras, also a Ph.D. clinical psychologist and couples therapist in Charlottesville, Virginia, says that longing for a sense of adulthood may draw many men toward marriage. "Marriage is a symbolic way for a man to step into adulthood," she says. "A society needs rituals for such transitions, and in our society, marriage is one of the few rituals we have to mark adulthood."

## Deep Psychology

Some experts argue that the yearning to marry and the choice of a mate are determined not just by evolutionary drives to procreate, brain chemistry, or social needs, but very much by what Sigmund Freud called the "Oedipus complex." According to Freud and his flock, a man's early relationship with his parents, particularly his mother, will affect his choice of mates on a powerful subconscious level.

Says Phyllis Koch-Sheras: "It could be argued that marriage is part of a man's subconscious psychological desire to reconnect with a woman in a deep and serious way, to form a bond with a woman like the one he hasn't had since birth."

According to Pennsylvania psychologist Ray Klein, Ed.D., consultant to MatchMaker International, "To some extent we all wind up unconsciously marrying our parents—one way or another. As children, we grow up looking for our parents' approval. That was the major motivator in our lives, which we can't just turn off when we become adults," he says. "That need for approval, and our parents' fashion of giving or withholding approval, becomes a model for all of our relationships later in life."

Robert Jaffe, Ph.D., a psychotherapist and relationships expert in Encino, California, says that when it comes to picking a spouse, men often wind up unconsciously following "scripts" passed on to them from their childhoods. "For example, a man whose father was the traditional protector/provider type will typically find himself attracted to women who project neediness," says Jaffe. "He isn't aware that he's doing this, but he's slipping right into the husband role that was created by his parents."

Robert M. Gordon, Ph.D., one of the most respected clinical psychologists in my hometown of Allentown, Pennsylvania, says that men are driven to particular women in response to their deep-seated sexual fantasies. "Men, for example, who envision themselves with sexually exciting and aggressive women may seek out mates to fulfill that fantasy. Unfortunately, they can be so led by the fantasy that they'll wind up with women who fit the bill (they're sexually aggressive) but may be wrong in all other regards (they're dim-witted, or moody).

"Other men," adds Gordon, "are afraid of their fantasies, and may set up psychological defenses to deny them. Some of those men might seek out prim and proper women (opposite to their fantasy girls), who may be just as wrong for them."

Where do fantasies come from? No one knows for sure. But Jim Sniechowski, Ph.D., author of *The New Intimacy: Discovering the Magic at the Heart of Your Differences* (Health Communications, 1997), says that fantasies are pivotal to the phenomenon we call *love at first sight*. "When we first meet the woman we're to marry, there's a sense of love at first sight. It's real, yes. But it really has little to do in a direct sense with the woman herself," he says.

"Rather, something about her—her body type, mannerisms, attitude, or personality—is serving as a trigger. We fall in love with the familiar. She may remind a man (most often subconsciously) of his mother—if not his mother, perhaps a favorite aunt, or Hollywood heartthrob when he was a kid," says Sniechowksi. "But there will be some connection to an ideal image of a woman that he has already formed."

## Following Religious Dictates

Believing more in the Bible than in Sigmund Freud, some marriage experts I talked with said that men are subconsciously led by God and religion to marry.

"Men in our society clearly get the message early on that marriage is the right thing to do. So there's a 'should,' an 'ought' that weighs into a man's decision to marry. Where does it come from? In large part, from religion," says the Reverend Kenneth Ferguson, pastor and teacher at the United Church of Christ on the campus of the University of Connecticut.

"I can't think of a single religious group that doesn't promote the institution of marriage," says Ferguson. "Every one of the holy books—the Old Testament, the New Testament, the Koran—advocates marriage. Is it any wonder then that marriage is such an ingrained tradition and popular option?"

And Rabbi Yechezkel Kornfeld, director of adult education at Chabad House in Seattle, Washington, adds, "In the Bible it clearly says that man and woman were originally created as one and then became separated. It also says that a man leaves his mother and father and cleaves to his wife. There is something in the spiritual dimension of every man that calls to be reunited with a woman, because togetherness was the original state of existence of human beings. In other words, every man has a drive to marry, whether conscious or subconscious, so to become jointed to a woman and thereby complete according to God's plan."

## Bending to Her Whim

A final group of thinkers says that regardless of men's many possible motivations to marry, guys would probably rarely take the plunge if not given a little shove by their girlfriends—and often they aren't even aware of being shoved.

"Marriage is totally against every drive a man has. It's a woman's invention. We women designed it for our biological and emotional needs. We tend to bring up marriage first, and we tend to bend men's arms to marry us," says Riki Robbins, Ph.D., relationships consultant and author of *Betrayed: How to Restore Sexual Trust* (Adams Media Group, 1998).

"In some cases we may fire off direct ultimatums ('marry me, or I'm history'). But other times, we issue more subtle ultimatums, so subtle men don't even realize they've received an ultimatum!" says Robbins. "The most common example: She'll say, 'I think we should start seeing other people.' She knows how important sexual exclusivity is to him, so she's betting he'll opt for marriage in order to get it. She's often right!"

Psychotherapist Jaffe agrees. "Men aren't as anxious about getting married as women are. Part of it is because men aren't so acculturated to think of marriage as a goal. Men also aren't on the same biological time clock. Because women feel more anxious than men, they are often the ones to initiate talk of marriage," says Jaffe. "Fairly often, they may begin to give subtle ultimatums to a reluctant boyfriend—they may, for example, start to pout or become less-willing date or sex partners."

Enough speculation as to why men marry. In Part Two, we'll hear from married and engaged guys themselves. But before we do, here is a bit of practical advice for single women who no longer want to be single. . . .

# 3

# WHAT EVERY SINGLE WOMAN SHOULD KNOW

*Twelve Tips for Groom Seekers*

Regardless of why men marry, certain predictable criteria enter into just about any man's choice of a bride. Here they are, based on input from hundreds of men: twelve things any and all marriage-minded women should keep in mind.

## 1 Be realistic.

Countless magazine articles, and some books, carry titles such as "You Can Make *Any Man* Your Love Slave!" Sorry, life doesn't work that way. Looks are very important to men. If you're cover-girl material, you'll have hordes of guys (but still not all) to pick from. If you're far less than photogenic, chances are that Leonardo DiCaprio will be taking a rain check. But regardless of your appearance, there's a man out there for you.

## 2 Don't smoke.

According to the application forms of 1,100 male clients of Matchmaker International of Pennsylvania, 99 percent of nonsmoking men (and about three-

### Where the Single Men Are

Just in case you've wondered, here, according to U.S. Census data, are the numbers of single men for every 100 single women in selected major American cities.

| | | | |
|---|---|---|---|
| Honolulu | 105 | Washington | 85 |
| Las Vegas | 105 | San Antonio | 82 |
| San Jose | 104 | Chicago | 82 |
| Los Angeles | 96 | Boston | 81 |
| San Francisco | 94 | Detroit | 80 |
| Houston | 93 | Miami | 78 |
| Seattle | 92 | Philadelphia | 78 |
| Dallas–Fort Worth | 88 | New York | 77 |

quarters of men today do *not* smoke) say they want a nonsmoking spouse. Many guys who do smoke say they, too, would prefer a nonsmoking wife and mother for their children.

## 3 Be happy.
Nine out of ten guys agree: a big smile is a huge turn-on.

## 4 Listen up.
Men want audiences. They crave to be heard, to share stories, to have the full attention of a woman. Ask him every night about his day.

## 5 Have a life.
Many men fear giving up theirs, and they're likely to sense that is what will happen if you start to give up yours. Men worry about getting smothered.

## 6 Stay fit.
Big may be beautiful, but few men opt for chunky dates. On the other hand, men aren't looking for Olive Oyl, either. Most guys are drawn to women of average weight, with some tone.

# 7 Play hard to get, but . . .

*Don't* play hard to get with the guy you have your eye
on! A man is most likely to fall in love with a woman
who plays hard to get with *other* men but who gives
the impression of being solely captivated by him. That
can be a hard act, but some women have it mastered.

# 8 Act loved.

You need to take it for granted that you are loved and
to act accordingly. Constantly doubting and questioning
a man's love makes you jealous and shrewish—turn-
offs on a par with bad breath and missing teeth. In
contrast, feeling loved makes you radiantly beautiful.

# 9 Cook him a meal.

It's been known to lure men into marriage. Just ask
Grandma. You think things have really changed that
much?

# 10 Leave your roots be.

Don't panic if you weren't born a blond. "I've found
that while blonds are more likely to catch a man's eye
on the street, most men opt for dark-haired women to

marry. They probably see the dark-haired woman as having more substance," says Sarah Ossey, president of Providence Matchmaking in New York City.

# 11 Feel sexy.

Sexual confidence sends out vibes that men can't help but react to.

# 12 Doll up your mother.

Yes, your worst fear is true! Men *do* look at your mother for clues of things to come. If she looks good, fix her up to look great and introduce them as soon as possible. If she's gone to pot, hide her until he's so madly in love with you that his radar is jammed.

# PART TWO

*Husband Talk*

# 4

# THE PURSUIT OF PLEASURE

*Guys Who Married for the Fun of It*

These guys married for friendship. They married for sex. They married to have someone to go to the movies with. Their top requirements for a mate: sexy, funny, adventurous.

I suppose that every man hopes to find pleasure in marriage. I expected it. I got it. Most men do. "The main source of happiness is having close, warm, and enduring relationships. And the main generator of such relationships is marriage and the family," writes David Popenoe, Ph.D., professor of sociology at Rutgers University, in his *Life Without Father* (Free Press, 1996). "Many studies of marriage and happiness have been

37

conducted over the years, and they invariably find a strong, positive association," he states. "In social surveys, fewer than 25 percent of unmarried adults but nearly 40 percent of married adults report being 'very happy.'"

Men who marry for pleasure tend to seek mates with whom they have much in common—for instance, a sense of humor. I don't know any man who doesn't relate to the famous kitchen scene in *Annie Hall*, where Woody Allen chases the lobster clumsily around the room, making wisecracks, while Annie titters away (as opposed to Woody's date from hell, who, under the same circumstances, stands there watching him, stone-faced).

Early in my relationship with Susan, when she was still in college, as a gag I would occasionally pick up one of those round, prickly things that fall from sycamore trees and drop it into her book bag for her to find later that day in class. She returned the joke by bringing it home and slipping it into one of my suit pockets for me to find the next day on the job. That was eighteen years ago. To this day, I'll be digging in my pocket for a quarter, a pen, or one of my keys, and out will come one of those round, prickly things.

Ed, a financial manager, told me that he finds pleasure in the fact that he and Eva have similar tastes in home decorating. Bob the psychologist told me that he enjoys sharing his interests about the human psyche with fiancée Beth. Computer whiz Ben told me that he really likes his and Ann's shared interests in medieval history and body art.

In the case of David M., the first man profiled in this chapter, he takes pleasure in knowing that he and Jan share a bunch of similar recreational interests, like snowmobiling, skiing, and enjoying music in the park.

# David M.
## *He enjoys an activity-filled marriage*

*Married in 1982, he and Jan live in rural Pennsylvania, where David works as a service technician for the local cable company and coaches Little League. They met on a blind date arranged by a work colleague of David's who was dating (and eventually married) Jan's sister. The year was 1976, and David and Jan were still in high school. Now in their late thirties, they have two boys, ages twelve and eight.*

I first saw her in her parents' house, standing in the kitchen. She was wearing jeans and had a cast on her arm, the result of a roller-skating accident. You never know with a blind date, but I saw her and I felt awfully glad to be there. She was pretty, prettier than any girl I'd dated before.

We went to the movies that first night, had a good time, and started seeing each other fairly regularly. It was about three and a half years before I proposed, but by then we both knew deep down that we'd be getting married. So when I asked her, it was in a very casual way. No big deal. "Want to get married?" That was it.

I was raised in a good family. We did lots of things together. My parents were always real happy, and their marriage was a part of that happiness. To me, marriage seemed like the right thing, the proper thing, the fun thing to do. It's definitely more fun spending your life with someone you really like, right?

Jan also came from a close-knit family that did lots of things together, and we've both followed in our parents' footsteps. We're big into birthday parties, family vacations, skiing together, snowmobiling, those sorts of things. Doing stuff together, going places, that's what makes the marriage for us. And no matter what we're doing—sitting on a bench, grabbing a few drinks, listening to a band—we enjoy each other's company.

## GROWING TOGETHER

### An $80 pair of sneakers!?

The children are a big part of our marriage. As they grow, the marriage grows. That's because raising kids is so full of challenges and adventures that things never get stale. It's a constant learning experience. Yesterday, Jeffrey came home and said he wanted an $80 pair of sneakers. What do we do? How do we handle that? I don't know yet, but it's something that Jan and I will need to figure out together.

# Adam

*Love me tender*

> *He and Penny were childhood friends and high school sweethearts. They married in 1981, in their early twenties. "My parents loved each other very much. I always saw marriage as something positive," says Adam. He and Penny ran a delicatessen for six years, but the business proved unprofitable. This interview took place shortly before the family moved from Pennsylvania to Wisconsin, where Adam was to begin his new job as food and beverage director at a large hotel. He is thirty-seven years old and enjoys fishing and motorcycling. The couple has a twelve-year-old boy and a seven-year-old girl.*

When I was ten years old, my mother would take me to the shoe store where Penny's father worked. He'd always say that I looked just like his daughter. It was true. If you look at pictures of us as kids, we looked very much alike.

Our romantic relationship began in high school, and within a year of dating, we were planning for a long future together. I proposed to her while on Christmas break from college. Finances were an issue, but I talked to my father, and he said, "If you wait till you can afford to get married, you never will." I proposed (on the couch in her parents' house). She accepted. We both went back to school and left our mothers to plan the wedding for that May.

There was no reason to play the field. I envisioned Penny as a wonderful mother and a terrific life mate. She was happy, funny, honest, and very much committed to the relationship.

My hunch about her committedness proved right on. Five years ago, I had an affair. It remained hidden until I had an emotional breakdown. I came apart at the seams and told Penny the whole thing. She felt violated and extremely hurt. But she was committed to salvaging our family, committed to not letting it all go out the door for a mistake I made. We were at the lowest point we ever were, but because Penny was willing, we worked together to analyze what happened and to grow from there.

The weekend after next we're heading to Las Vegas, to the Graceland Chapel, where Penny and I will renew our wedding vows with the help of an Elvis impersonator!

## SWEET REUNION

### Doing Cyrano de Bergerac proud

In high school I was dating a friend of hers, and she was dating a friend of mine, but eyes would wander. I started to try to woo her, but she wanted only a platonic relationship. Then, in her senior year, she went to Israel for a semester, and I wrote her *every single day*. That's when the metamorphosis occurred. She started writing me back, and over the weeks, the tone of her responses began to change. When she came back, we embraced like never before. It went from a friendly hug to an intimate hug to a kiss. I can remember very clearly the lightheadedness, my heart jumping into my throat, and my palms sweating. I'd been looking forward to that moment for a long time. From that point on, we were "Adam and Penny."

# Alex
*Enough commuting, already*

> *He is thirty-five years old and works as the*
> *director of environmental management of a*
> *New England utility company. He and Tara*

*have been married for six years. They have a*
*boy, one year old.*

She worked for an analytical lab, and I was with an environmental consulting firm. We had talked on the phone, and I thought she had a great phone voice. I saw her at the lab—light blond hair, big blue eyes, nice big smile, down-to-earth, and happy. Very happy.

I was convinced that a girl with her looks and personality would have a boyfriend. It took me two weeks to get up the nerve to ask her out to dinner! She said she was busy but that she'd like to later in the week. We made plans and went out for Mexican food. There was no shortage of conversation. Two days later, I asked her out again.

We saw each other almost every day after that second date—but she had already decided to move back to San Francisco, which would leave us a continent apart. I drove part of the trip with her. We then did the coast-to-coast commute thing for the next two years. Meanwhile, I was talking the whole time about moving out to California with her. But in 1990, I was offered a great new job in the East, and I couldn't pass it up.

She was going to Greece to see a friend. I decided to fly over and meet her there. I knew that something had to be done if I was going to stay on the East Coast and maintain the relationship, which I definitely wanted to do. She wasn't going to move back to New

England without a commitment. That was sure. So I had to decide. I thought of how much I enjoyed doing things with her—hiking, going to musicals, traveling, talking. To let her slip away would be awful! I proposed to her in Greece—in a letter. We were married a year later.

Having to cooperate to work out problems and make decisions can be hard. At times it can be very hard. But for the most part, marriage has been real easy and comfortable. I'm in this for the long haul. She is really great. You should see her as a mom!

# Fred

## *He appreciates his "long chain"*

*He was twenty-four when he met Heather in 1989. She was sixteen. He far from objected when, the night they were introduced, she pulled him close by the back of his head and planted a long, open kiss on his mouth. "I didn't know how young she was; I thought she was eighteen or nineteen." Despite the initial objections of her parents (because of the age difference), the two continued dating and moved in together in 1994. "We plan to marry just as soon as we have enough money for the wedding," says Fred. This conversation took*

*place at a Mexican restaurant in the same*
*strip mall where Fred works in the warehouse*
*of a chain furniture store.*

I consider us already married, really. The wedding will be just a nice thing, a good party, and I love good parties with family and friends. Then we'll be able to say we're married, and that'll be nice, too. Marriage is all about image. And cheaper insurance. Other than that, when we're married, things will all be the same. She'll just have a ring on her finger.

Why Heather? She is a good person, very thoughtful. You tell her a story, and she'll listen. She stands behind me. She also understands that we're both individuals, and she keeps me on a long chain, lets me do what I want to do. Like when I got this haircut [cropped short in front, with a long tail at the nape], she wasn't crazy about it, but she let me do it. And now I'm telling her that I'm getting a tattoo [the emblem of his favorite hockey team on the back of the calf], and she says OK.

Heather and I are true to each other. There's trust there. Like we go to the water park and there are these hot chicks in red, white, and blue bikinis. I check them out, and I say, "Heather, look at that—I got to do my patriotic duty and salute them," and she'll make a face. So I say, "Hey, you'd rather have me looking at girls than looking at guys, right?" I can goof around with her like that, because we're true to each other.

# Bob M.
## *No more "serial dating"*

> *A busy psychoanalyst who enjoys sailing, tennis, and quick conversation, he dated more than three hundred women in the fifteen years following his divorce. "I enjoy the company of women," he says. "I felt that if I met the woman of my dreams, fine. If not, I was just going to enjoy dating." He did meet the woman of his dreams. Her name is Beth. The two are living together, planning to wed in six months. Bob has a teenage son and daughter. Beth, also once divorced, has a seven-year-old daughter. Bob is fifty.*

Right after my divorce, I was anxious to remarry. But being a psychoanalyst, and in my midthirties, I knew that finding the right woman would require both hard work and chance, so I set out to do a lot of dating. I answered a bunch of personal ads, attended singles dances, went out on blind dates . . . Any avenue that was ethical, I tried.

One of the personal ads I answered said "Pretty, thin woman, forty, mom with small child" (a lot of men see a kid as baggage, but not me). I called her up. She had a very sexy voice. We spoke for over an hour, connected well, and decided to meet a few days later, at a restaurant. In the meantime, she had reluctantly agreed to send me her photo, in which she appeared kind of cute.

She looked a thousand times better in person! We flirted heavily. I wanted to take her to bed right away! I asked her out again for the following Sunday. On that date, she scared me a little, talking about her failed relationships. History repeats. I might have fled, but she wasn't at all defensive, and that impressed me. It's easy to blame all past relationship problems on the other people. Beth didn't do that. She wasn't blind to her own psychological issues. (She has since gone into analysis and is working through those issues beautifully.)

My dream was to marry my best friend, and that is what I'll be doing. Beth and I laugh together often. Sex is great. And when I need help, she's a good therapist, filling the role for me that I fill with so many others. I'm very glad to be getting married, and I'm especially glad that Beth's daughter, Iris, is part of the picture. I've had fun as a single man. I had a sex life most men would dream of. But family is what I *really* want.

## MOVING IN CLOSER

### A tale of two cats

She had cats. I'm allergic. In fact, two years before I responded to her personal ad, she had answered one of mine. We spoke, I liked the sound of her voice, but I nixed her because of those cats. This time around, it was still an obstacle to overcome. After a few months of dating, we started talking about moving in together. I approached the subject gingerly, asking if perhaps we might keep the cats in a separate area of the house. We didn't need to. She decided to get rid of the animals. As her mother would say, "*That's* when I knew the relationship was serious."

# "Balloons"

## *Marriage is no laughing matter*

*"The one thing I learned at Ringling Brothers is that the more different you are from the person under the makeup, the better the clown. Similarly, the more different you are from your mate, the better the family," he says. "Balloons," whose real name is Neal, spent several years with the circus and now*

*works as a self-employed clown. He is thirty-seven years old and has been married to Terry since 1984. They have one daughter and many animals, including three dogs, a bunny, a dove, and a llama named Ama.*

I was working weekdays at this Carvel [an ice cream shop] three or four doors down from the Woolworth's where my buddy, John, was manager. Terry worked at the Woolworth's across the river, but the two of them would get together sometimes to do inventory. John was keen on her, but he figured it wouldn't be good business practice to ask her out. So I did.

Our first date was to go see the play *Carnival*, which I had helped direct, at the local high school. We went out in my old Dodge van that was painted up with "Balloons the Clown" all over it. That date went well, as did the next few, but I don't think I really started to feel that she was Miss Right until one summer day when we went to the fair and she won a live bunny rabbit. I like the way she relates to animals (although she doesn't much like my dove).

We got engaged on April 1, 1983, about a year after we met. I was looking for a permanent partnership and the security that it brings. In the short run, dating a different girl every week sounds great. But in the long run, the disadvantages—the broken hearts, the risk of venereal disease, the uncertainties—start to outweigh the advantages.

Terry and I make such a good couple mostly because we're so different. Opposites attract—that's one of those old sayings that really makes sense. She likes to be at home; I like to go out. She likes goofy vegetables like asparagus and broccoli; I like snow cones. I buy things like electronic equipment on impulse; she's more thrifty. I like loud colors; she likes somber.

Are there any things we have in common? We both like blue. And kids. And animals.

## ON BENDED KNEE

### Park-'n'-propose

We went to the theater in that old van of mine. What Terry didn't know was that earlier that day I had bought a new car, a Dodge Omni. While we were at the theater, I had my Mom take away the van and park the new car in its place. So when we got to the parking spot, Terry gasped when she saw the van missing. Then she looked at the car that had taken its place and noticed what was written in big letters on the window: "Surprise Enax!" (Enax is her nickname.) We got into the car, and I asked her to check out the glove compartment, where I had stashed the ring. She found it and looked shocked. I said, "So, will 'ya?" She said, "Yes."

# Chris

*She's "perfect"*

> *He's a National Guardsman, a warehouse*
> *laborer, and a guitar player into alternative*
> *rock and heavy metal. He first spotted Larissa*
> *in November 1993 at an ice-skating rink. "I*
> *saw her and thought that I just had to get to*
> *meet her. Then I found out she was friends*
> *with my friend, and I went 'wow,'" he says.*
> *Chris and Larissa were both sixteen at the*
> *time. They got engaged to be married a little*
> *over three years later, several months before*
> *this interview.*

I never thought about marriage till we were both eighteen. I had signed up for the army, and I left on basic training for five and a half months. I was expecting Larissa to go out with her friends and have fun. But every time I called her, she was always home. It was like a part of her was missing when I was gone. And with her gone from my side, it was like a part of me was missing.

We're great together. We're best friends. And I don't want anything to change that. I see marriage as a way to keep things as they are. We just got an apartment together to make sure that we can live together.

My biggest fear is that everybody keeps telling us we're so young. In the back of my mind, I have to think maybe they're right. But instinctually, I feel I'm right and that we're going to have a great marriage.

I haven't had many relationships, but she's all I could ever need. She's caring, loyal, funny, smart . . . In a word, *perfect*. And I don't think I'll ever get bored with her. She's too full of surprises. Every day she surprises me. For instance, she'll beat me home from work and have dinner ready with a present on the table for me. If I ever started to get bored, I'd tell her, and I know she'd do anything. Like sexually, if I wanted a blond or a redhead, she'd dye her hair. If I wanted something more exotic, she'd role-play. She can be really wild, but she looks *so* innocent. I take her home to Mother, and Mother is awfully impressed—but if Mother only knew!

## ON BENDED KNEE

**As the ball dropped . . .**

On New Year's Eve, just before midnight, as 1997 was about to begin, that's when I popped the question. We were at a party at my cousin's house. My whole family was there, and hers, too. A minute before the big ball dropped on TV, I got down on one knee. She thought I was just getting down to tie my shoe. I brought out the little black box with the ring and asked her to marry me. Her first reaction was to say, "Oh, shit, no!" and then she turned away and started to cry. I got plenty nervous! But after about three seconds she turned back around and said, "Yes."

# Jaymie
*Moved by magic*

> *He and Jean had an on-again, off-again relationship from the time they met in high school to the time he proposed, thirteen years later. Jaymie is thirty-seven, an attorney. He and Jean have three children.*

We dated through high school and college. She dated other men. I dated other women. During law school I was actually given ultimatums by two other women who wanted to marry me. (Interestingly, only weeks apart!) No way, I thought. I wasn't going to marry anyone but Jean. I was just waiting until after I graduated before I proposed.

What was it about Jean? Oh, I suppose I could talk about how she's attractive, and has a great personality, and wasn't "clingy" like other women. But the truth is, I don't really know. That's the magic. I just didn't feel that same magic with any other woman. Some people tell me Jean looks a lot like my mom, but I've never seen that. They're both tall and slight, but that's about the only similarity as far as I'm concerned.

I asked her to marry me at her parents' farm. It was around Christmas, and she always got sick from stress around Christmas because she was working in retail. Anyway, I proposed, she said yes, and then she promptly ran to throw up. While she was doing that, I went to see her father, who was in the chicken coop, and asked for his permission and blessing. He agreed, we had some Scotch, and that was that.

## REFLECTIONS

### Lust isn't enough

A lot of guys, particularly younger ones, are apt to marry out of lust. There's nothing wrong with lust—far from it. But in this day and age, you don't need to get married to satisfy sexual urges. Marriage should be founded on other things, like friendship, mutual respect, and shared life goals. I believe what my great-grandfather used to say—"You got to be the same type of wood."

# John C.

## *A thoroughly sober devotion*

> *He first saw Michele walking down New York's*
> *Broadway. "It was October 1991. I was in this*
> *phone booth, leaving a message for a friend,*
> *looking out onto the street, and before my eyes*
> *comes this perfectly beautiful young woman.*
> *She was wearing jeans and a black leather*
> *jacket, smiling broadly. She was perfectly*
> *gorgeous," he says. "She also had that*
> *hydraulic tush movement that men like so*
> *much. I decided to follow her." John writes*
> *pulp fiction, collects rare books and coins, and*
> *works as the manager of a chain bookstore. He*
> *is thirty-nine years old.*

I'm not used to accosting women on the street, and I
never would have—but fate came into play. I was hanging back about fifty feet in her wake when she turns
into a door. I recognized it as an AA (Alcoholics Anony-
mous) meeting right off the bat. I'm a recovering alco-
holic myself, and I was no stranger to the meetings. I
walked in and sat down along the side wall, where I
could see Michele from an angle, and pretended to listen to the speaker. I'm admiring her when her eyes
drifted toward me. She just looked at me as natural as
can be and smiled.

Michele spoke at the meeting. You could tell by the timbre of her voice that she was intelligent. And I could see that her fingers were naked, no wedding ring. I also learned that she was five years recovering, which made her available. (There are heavy taboos in AA about getting sexual with people who are recovering for less than a year—they're too vulnerable.) I thought, my God, I'm in love. I planned to attend all the local AA meetings, hoping to run into her again. It didn't take long. The next meeting I went to, there she was. "Hi, I'm John," I said. "I've seen you at a couple of meetings, and I just wanted to introduce myself."

Best move I ever made—and marrying her was the best thing I ever did for myself. She's the most gracious and decent person I've ever known, bereft of malice. And we have so much in common that we're almost like male and female versions of the same person. We're very much in love but not blinded by our passions or romantic ideations. I was smitten when I first saw her on the street; I still am.

## ON BENDED KNEE

### A perfect picture

I took her to the Conservatory Gardens in Central Park on the most perfect Sunday in May, and while we stood under the old ironwork wisteria pergola overlooking the mayflowers, I slipped her my mother's

mother's mother's mother's diamond engagement ring.
She was flattered, said I did right by her, did it right.

# Brian
*Seduced by Brahms*

> *Raised in London, England, he is fifty-two*
> *years old and has been married since 1974.*
> *He works as a computer programmer for an*
> *international humanitarian association, plays*
> *squash, and enjoys classical music. Brian and*
> *his wife, Anna, live in Geneva, Switzerland.*
> *They have two children.*

I met her in the flat of my friend Stuart. He had picked
me up at the Geneva airport that afternoon and said
that he had invited a few friends to join us for dinner,
Anna among them. Stuart got to know Anna because
she was secretary to the secretary general of one of the
organizations here in Geneva, and Stuart was with the
British delegation to the United Nations. Their paths
crossed at various functions.

When I first saw her, she was smiling, chatting,
being introduced by my old school friend to the rest of
us, saying, "Pleased to meet you! Hello!" with a lovely

smile on her face. Anna and I sat opposite at dinner and talked mostly to each other. After the meal, we all went back to her place for coffee.

The following day I continued on to Rome. I rang Anna in her office from down there, and she joked about having forgotten me. But yes, she might be free in a week when I planned on stopping once more in Geneva on my way back to London. Much later, the woman Anna shared an office with at the time gave a great impersonation of that particular conversation, going from being wildly enthusiastic with her hand on the mouthpiece ("It's him! It's him!") to cool and calm while actually talking with me!

We had our first actual date that following week. Seven weeks later, I dropped to my knee.

Why did I want her as my wife? Everything about her seemed perfect. She was beautiful, well educated, fun loving, independent, no ties, and the right age. She was also "exotic" in that she came from a different culture (Swedish), she had no silly social hang-ups, she spoke an impressive number of languages, she was well organized, and—perhaps most important—she had Brahms's *German Requiem* in her record collection!

Geography was the only impediment we had to marriage (I was living in England), but as I had a transportable skill (programming), I looked around in

Geneva and found a job there. We were engaged seven months before we married.

## ON BENDED KNEE

**Off with the bloody TV**

Back from the pub to my flat, "midnight" movie on the television, and I suddenly found myself on my knees. I proposed and she just gave me a lovely smile. "Yes, of course," was the reply. "Oh!" I said. "Don't you want to think about it a bit?" "No, I'm sure," she said. "Right, well," I started, not sure what happens next at these times. "What shall we do now?" "Well, you could turn that bloody television off," she suggested with the same sweet smile. Then we went to the kitchen and retrieved the champagne from the fridge.

# Kermit

*Sweetly reminiscing*

*A former president of several public apparel companies, he is in his late seventies.*

It was January 5, 1946. I was still in the army. We met at a hotel in Lakewood, New Jersey, while I was being mustered out from Camp Kilmer. We made a date for the following week. It was on her birthday. In a month or so we were engaged (I proposed on Valentine's Day), and we married three months later.

She was a beautiful, tall blond with blue eyes and a size-eight figure. More importantly, we felt enormous love for one another that grew over the forty-eight years we were together. She died two years ago. How I miss the conversations and her laughter. I am devastated, still.

I've been living with a lovely widow for the past year and a half, but I have no plans to marry again.

# Scott W.
*Roommates . . . forever*

> *They were buddies in college, kept in touch afterward, even shared an apartment for two years while juggling separate love relationships. Then Scott and Susan kissed for the first time—twelve years after meeting. "The best kiss I ever had," he says. "From that moment on, that was it. We knew we were meant for each other." Scott is thirty-six years old, raised in California, works as a*

*hydrogeologist (groundwater expert), and
enjoys hiking, cycling, and gardening.*

We had this wonderful friendship. We were very protective of each other, in a sibling kind of way. Parents and friends said we were perfect together and should be a couple. But we didn't want to jeopardize what we had. We both knew of other friendships that had gotten romantic and then had blown apart. I think we just needed a push to take the big risk. That push came when she left.

Susan had been dating this guy who was going to France to work for about six months, and he asked her to come with him. After some initial hesitation, she went. (To see if he was the right one, she said.) We sent letters and postcards back and forth, with the occasional call. Finally, I asked about visiting. I suggested my girlfriend and I come over, but Susan would have nothing to do with that! Well, I certainly did not want to be the "third wheel" with her and her boyfriend, and I told her so. There was only one way around this problem. I broke up with my girlfriend, she broke up with her boyfriend, and that cleared our way.

I flew to Zurich and took the train to Bern, where I met Susan coming off a train from Mulhouse, France. From there we traveled throughout Switzerland by train for ten days, hiking our way through the country, but sleeping in separate beds and not talking about the "situation" or "us" at all. Then, in the room where we were staying, the night before we were leaving Europe, we kissed for the first time.

It had been a long time coming. It was great! Nothing awkward about it. We went back to San Francisco, where we lived for another two years—this time as a couple—before we married. We became engaged in November 1993 and were married in May 1994. Why marriage? There was no other woman that I had ever met with whom I was so comfortable, both as a friend and romantic partner. There are so many things I love about her but perhaps nothing more than her passion for getting something done right once she sets her sights on it . . . be it a hobby, a hill to climb, or being the best mother she can be to our little girl.

## ON BENDED KNEE

**Love, mountain style**

It was her birthday, and she surprised me with a plane ride to Oregon for a weekend of hiking in the Cascades and seeing some Shakespeare. Well, I surprised her by proposing during one of our hikes. We had paused for a rest near this great overview, and I pulled out the ring and asked her to marry me. Her first response was to look at the ring and say, "It's sooo

cute! It looks just like one of the rings in those adver-
tisements!" (We later laughed about that.) Then, of
course, she said, "Yes!"

# R.G.
*Go Gators!*

> *He first saw his future wife sitting at a*
> *Teletype machine. They worked for the same*
> *company. He was a supervisor, and she had*
> *just come in from another department. At the*
> *time, 1987, R.G. was fifty. He and Theresa*
> *were married three years later.*

She was wearing nice blue jeans with an orange University of Florida Gator logo on the back pocket, and a
white pullover shirt with the University of Florida logo
on the breast. Probably coincidence, because it was her
first day working for me and I'm known to be a rabid
Gator fan, right?! I approached her to introduce myself.
She started to stand, and I told her to keep her seat.

The first thing that struck me was her face. She had
classic Slovak looks—dark eyes, high cheekbones, chis-
eled features. My first impression was, "Now, that is
one of the most beautiful women I've ever seen." She
also had a knockout figure—the body I have always
admired in a woman: rounded (not fat, as in Rubin's

women, but soft) with a smallish but shapely bust—although I couldn't tell this at first sight, because, as I said, she was sitting.

Our first date was to a University of Florida football game. I rented two rooms at a motel (in Gainesville). We went to the game and then supper. It went just fine.

After two marriages, I was thinking I'd remain single. But Theresa changed that. She has a sense of humor, intelligence, determination, a strong sense of right and wrong, and, like me, a willingness to please. Others laugh when we try to decide on something, because each of us pushes to please the other. For example, I'd rather go to a community theater play because I know how much she enjoys them; but she'll suggest a baseball game, although the game confuses the hell out of her, because she knows I'm a baseball nut.

We have an excellent marriage and have never had an argument, or even a cross word, and we've known each other for more than ten years.

## Michael O.
*He takes his serve*

> *"I've always wanted to get married and have a family. But during more than twenty years of dating, I kept worrying that there was*

*someone better out there. This time, however, I*
*was ready because Alex is the right person,"*
*he says. Michael works as a cook in a well-*
*known New York delicatessen and helps run a*
*recreational volleyball league. He is forty*
*years old, and he and Alex have been married*
*for two years. They are trying to have a child.*

She came to play at an outdoor volleyball game. She was with a couple of her friends, and I have to admit she wasn't the first one I noticed. One of her friends was more attention-getting physically, but I soon discovered that friend was a little nuts.

Our first date was several weeks after the game. We went out for Chinese food and a movie. I'd say we hit it off very well, and I felt very comfortable talking to her. We had a good-night kiss, and that went well too!

I proposed after about a year and a half. It was a surprise to her because even though we'd talked about marriage, she wasn't yet divorced. She assumed I'd wait until her papers were final to make any decisions about marriage. We had talked about my long-standing fear/hope that there might be that more-perfect person around the corner, and I knew that my honesty both pleased and worried her. She'd been dumped uncere-moniously by her ex-husband with no explanation, and she was scared of that happening again. She still is. So

I have to remind her every so often that I am sure I made the right choice.

How do I know? On a superficial level, we both enjoy volleyball, the outdoors, reading, "Star Trek," good food, TV, and going to the movies. But more important is that we share a similar value and belief system and outlook on life and our future. We believe in honesty and loyalty. We're both easygoing, not compulsive, and have similar senses of humor. We have a great relationship that continues to get better.

## ON BENDED KNEE

### South of the border

We went on a vacation to Cancun in April 1994. I had snuck the ring into my luggage, and on the second day there we started to get dressed for dinner. I had brought a tuxedo shirt, just for kicks (she thought), and I put it on. When she saw that, she decided to change and dress up a little too. So we went down to the hotel's outdoor restaurant and sat down. It was early. We were the only people there. The waiters were very attentive, even hovering. We decided to live dangerously and ordered Mexican wine (don't do it!). It was awful. After a glass or two, I took the bull by the horns and got off my chair and down on one knee. She looked alarmed and happy all at once. I could barely get the words out; I said something about wanting to spend the rest of my life with her. Her immediate response was, "Are you sure?" When I said yes, she said yes. We both cried, as the waiters watched with huge smiles on their faces.

# Mark

## *In love with a quirk*

> *A self-described "middle-aged hippy," Mark still sports the long hair and swooping mustache he did as a student in the 1960s. He first met Catherine (Cat) when he was thirty-four, a few years after he returned from his army stint in Vietnam. They wed four months later. Mark runs a home-inspection business, and Cat is a landscape designer.*

I had been with many, many women, a few men, and even, when I was a teenager, an occasional farm animal. [Mark grew up on a farm in Maine, miles from anything.] No kidding. (Laughs.) Cat was the first woman, or *anything* for that matter, that I never got bored with—not intellectually, not sexually. Oh, she's quirky. Wanted to get married in cowboy boots. Swears like a trucker. Damn near shoots my head off if I don't bring her flowers every day. But that's what makes Cat Cat. And, I suppose, it's that quirkiness, and her acceptance of my quirkiness, that makes us click.

# Tony C.
## *Beyond Heaven's Gate*

> *Married twice before. Both earlier marriages*
> *wound up in divorce. At age forty-four, says*
> *Tony, "I had lost all hope." Then he met Kathy.*

I know it's a cliché to say it was "love at first sight," but those are really the only words I can use. I was working at Heaven's Gate, feeling kind of low that night. [Heaven's Gate is a nightclub where Tony is both the manager and operates the food concession.] Kathy walked up and asked me why I wasn't smiling. It wasn't like a pickup line or anything. She was just curious.

Up to that point I'd been praying to meet the right one—but I never really thought it would happen, not at my age, not after two failed marriages.

What was it about Kathy? I see a lot of girls in my business. A lot of them are kind of trashy. She was different. The way she comes on. There's a sense of, I don't know, purity. And then we started talking and had so much in common. Like hiking, and nice dinners with a little wine. And animals. She has a Rottweiler and two cats. I love her animals.

After a month of seeing Kathy, we spent the night together. Oh. It was great. You know, guys always walk up to me and say, "Tony, man, you must get laid all the time." But it ain't true. It had been a *long* time. (Laughs.) That's one thing great now about being married, knowing I can have sex when I want it.

Sex though isn't the most important thing. Communication is what's most important. I don't hide anything from Kathy, and I don't think she hides anything from me. Any problems we have—hey—we talk about it. We're totally honest with each other. I never had that with any of my past relationships.

## ON BENDED KNEE

### A casual approach

The first time we ever talked marriage? It was about a month after we met, a few days after we spent our first night together. Kathy came into the club for happy hour. I was just walking around on the job, checking up on things, and I saw her alone. So I walked up, and I said, "Would you marry me?" She said, "Yes." I've been on this crazy high ever since.

# Thomas
## *Seven is his lucky number*

> *He says he wasn't looking for wife number seven*
> *when he fell for the married woman, twenty-four*
> *years his junior, who lived across the street. He*
> *is in his midfifties, and works as an office assist-*
> *ant for the county government. He and Lena*
> *were married in 1993. Thomas has four children*
> *from previous marriages and twelve stepchild-*
> *ren, including one stepdaughter with Lena.*

I was pretty much set against any more tries. I had
been divorced for a little over a year. A girl I'd been living with for nearly a year had moved out in the middle of the night. Came home in the morning to find the
house a disaster. Her, her kids, the furniture, all gone.
I decided to hell with women and spent my time working, learning computers, and trying to improve my
bass-fishing skills. (Still haven't done that!)

One day, I was invited to a neighbor's house to play
table tennis. Lena was wearing a T-shirt two times too
big for her and a pair of baggy shorts. We played a
game and she couldn't return the ball. (She admitted
later that the reason she couldn't was she was too busy
checking me out.) We didn't speak to each other for a
week after that. Then one night I'm sitting outside, and

she comes walking down her drive. I thought she was coming over to me. I walked down to meet her, but she angled off down the street. I realized that she had maneuvered into a position where her husband couldn't see her from the house. She passed me a slip of paper that told me to call her.

We started to have a relationship, which wasn't easy. I didn't have a telephone, so I had to go to a pay phone at a nearby store. Then, of course, there was the problem of working around her husband's schedule. He was a jealous guy. Once he came over to confront me. He had found the house key I'd given to Lena. I made like a politician, denying everything. "I have no idea what she's doing with that key," I said.

Despite the obstacles, Lena and I got to know each other well. The initial attraction was all physical, for both of us, but because we were forced to do a lot of talking on the phone, we were able to slow down and look at each other for who we were. We found that despite our age difference we both felt the same about most things in life. I was impressed with her good sense and levelheadedness.

## ON BENDED KNEE

### Just the right moment

It was several months after her divorce. A little over a year after we met. We were living together. I had mentioned on several occasions that we should get married, not really a proposal. Finally, one day she passingly remarked that if we were going to get married we'd better go do it before she changed her mind. Later that week we went to the courthouse and did it.

# Wayne B.
*Saving a pooch*

> *He is in his late forties, works by day as an OB-GYN, and by night as an aspiring mystery novelist. He and Lyndy were married in 1978. They have two children.*

When I first met her, she was a lab technician and I was a grad student trying to find a home for a dog that some neighbor lady, for no good reason, wanted to have killed. Lyndy wore a white coat and said no to the dog, yes to lunch. It's all kind of a blur now, it was so long ago. To be honest, I guess I found her interesting, and I remember just having gotten paid so I had cash in my pocket, but what I remember most about that day is that blasted dog. (Yes, I *did* find it a home.)

Lyndy and I dated for about nine months before I brought up marriage. I'd been badly burned in a previous divorce, and I really doubted I'd ever marry again. But I was awfully taken by Lyndy, in large part by her kindness; she hasn't a mean bone in her body. And she's also got brains—lots of 'em—and nice skin!

Our marriage has been wonderful. What I like best is raising the kids together and the solid, day-in, day-out companionship. Lyndy is someone I can talk to about things that I couldn't talk about to anyone else in the whole world.

## ON BENDED KNEE

### An interrupted sentence

One day we were just goofing off and I suggested marriage as a *possibility*. Just something to *consider*. I think I said, "Look, I don't want you to feel that you need to make a decision right away, but . . ." And to my great surprise, before I could even finish my sentence, she said, "Yes!"

# 5

# EXERCISES IN PRAGMATISM

*They Saw Marriage as a Sensible Gig*

ot that these guys didn't marry for pleasure, but each also had some eminently practical reason for tying the knot. English philosopher Francis Bacon realized that pragmatism is part of marriage when he wrote, "Wives are young men's mistresses, companions for middle age, and old men's nurses."

I didn't have the opportunity to talk with Bacon, because he's been dead for four hundred years, but I did talk with John Gray, Ph.D., relationships expert and author of (gadzillions of copies of) the "Venus and Mars" books. Gray said, "It may be politically incorrect to even talk about this, but the truth is that wives still do most of the cooking in our world. Many men have said to me that they first fell in love with their future wife after she made a wonderful meal."

Psychologist Peter Sheras mentions another practical reason men marry: "A wife offers a man a standing audience. Men find it very validating to have someone who will pay them attention, listen to their stories, laugh at their jokes, and look to them for guidance and advice. Men just like to pontificate," he says. "I'd say it's partly for this reason that men tend to marry younger women, who will look up to them."

In my survey I found some men who mentioned cooking, others who admitted they like to talk and be listened to, and quite a few others who said marriage was a practical way to escape the hassles and expense of dating, including the specter of AIDS.

In the case of the first man profiled in this chapter, Bernie, who owns one of my favorite Italian restaurants (LoBaido's), he found not only a wife, but a business partner.

# Bernie
*Love à la carte*

> *Owning and operating an upscale Italian*
> *restaurant leaves him no time for leisure, but*

*Bernie says he's a happy man. Maribeth, his*
*wife of ten years, is often at his side running*
*the "store," as Bernie calls it. Born and raised*
*in Brooklyn, he moved to Allentown,*
*Pennsylvania, with his family when he was*
*nineteen. He is now thirty-two years old. This*
*interview took place late one night as the last*
*customers were finishing their plates.*

We were both working at the G. W. Motorlodge when
we met. I was waitering, she was at the front desk. I
remember seeing her and saying to myself, "Wow—
that's a beautiful girl." The first time I approached her
was to get my paycheck. She asked me where my
(Brooklyn) accent was from. She was a country girl,
very innocent and sort of backward. I liked that. She
also reminded me of an ex-girlfriend, but I never told
her so!

We started dating, and within a year or so, I proposed. I come from an Italian Catholic family. You
marry. You have kids. You start a business. That's what
you do.

Maribeth is warm, kind, intelligent, a risk taker,
and a bit temperamental. Not like me; I'm more calm
and conservative. We balance each other in some ways.
In other ways, we're just alike. For example, we're
both very hard workers.

Maribeth raises our three kids, does all the books, waitresses, helps plan the menus. Meanwhile, I'm putting in fifteen-to-seventeen-hour days in the kitchen. The stress of the restaurant business is something a lot of marriages couldn't survive. But we do, because we both know what kind of people we are, and we share the same dreams. We want to have a nice home, and we want good lives for our kids. We want to see them grow, go to college, and become assets to the community.

## ON BENDED KNEE

### Oops—one small thing forgotten

We were in the attic of my sister's house, where Maribeth was living to save money. I brought up the engagement ring. I told her I loved her and wanted to marry her. She starting crying. We went and told her family, and they were all really happy. With my family, it wasn't so easy. Sicilian tradition holds that the son should ask his father, and I didn't do that. Dad wasn't very pleased. But he forgave.

# David Q.

*Romance on the roof*

> *He is thirty-nine years old, the minister of a United Church of Christ congregation. He and*

*Anne met in 1978 in a college history class taught by a professor with Marxist leanings they called "Fred the Red." Married in November 1982, they have a twelve-year-old girl and an eight-year-old boy. Anne is an attorney in private practice.*

I was twenty. We hooked up with a friend of Anne's to go up to Connecticut to protest the launching of a Trident nuclear submarine. Up till then, we hadn't really spoken much. At the end of the weekend, as we were splitting up to head home, she asked me out for a beer. Oh my God, I was scared to death! All through college I had only had one date, I was so afraid of the opposite sex. I told her I was busy. So we never dated.

She soon left Philadelphia to attend law school in Washington, D.C., and we corresponded a bit. A year later, in May 1980, I finished college and I went down to Washington to do church volunteer work with the homeless. I got up the nerve to call Anne to ask her if she wanted to go out—but I wasn't really expecting her to say yes!

We started seeing each other on and off for about a year and a half. By that time, she was starting to think about what she was going to do, where she was going to go after graduating law school. She asked me point-blank one day whether she should count me into her plans. I was paralyzed. I felt like I was at the edge of a cliff and didn't know whether to jump. I mumbled something that probably made no sense.

She said, "Well, that's not good enough." And she turned around and left me. For a week I was miserable. My co-workers saw me moping around, and they encouraged me to call her. I did. Anne and I got together and wound up on the roof of the church. It was very hard for me, but I told her, "I love you. I want to be with you." We were back in a relationship and sort of bumbled from there into getting engaged and then married. There was never a formal proposal.

Marriage for me wasn't even in question. It was what everybody did, a natural part of life. And although I didn't have a lot of experience in relationships, I sensed that Anne was the one. She was beautiful, intelligent, thoughtful, and had both a serious side and a fun side. She also had a gentle side that appealed to me.

We've been married fifteen years now. I suppose I have the same "what if? . . ." questions from time to time that most other men have. That's not like having regrets. And it doesn't mean I'm not happy. I am. But I do think if I had played the field longer, I might have been more mature in my dealings with Anne. Well, one of the advantages of my job is that I get to hear others talk about their marriages. I still learn a lot from that.

# Joe

*Once upon a time . . .*

> *His relationship with Ginger has been "like a*
> *fairy tale," he says. Joe is forty years old, a*
> *partner in a law firm, coach to his and*
> *Ginger's eight-year-old son's baseball team,*
> *and also coach to their six-year-old daughter's*
> *soccer team. He and Ginger met in 1984 and*
> *married in 1985. It was a second marriage for*
> *both.*

We met at a Christmas party given by mutual friends who thought we might hit it off. I was excited to meet her partly because of her name—*Ginger*. (It might have been the "Gilligan's Island" thing.) Seeing her, I wasn't disappointed. She had long, blond hair and a nice figure with small breasts (I'm more a butt than a breast man). She also had braces on both her top and bottom teeth! You wouldn't think you could be smitten by someone in braces, but that didn't matter to me.

I wasn't looking to get into a relationship. I was just coming out of my divorce, and I figured I needed some time. But Ginger and I really hit it off. We talked that first night about where we used to take family vacations as kids, and it turned out we went to the same

New Jersey beach. That was only the start of the things we had in common. There was, I felt, a real rapport. The friends who had the party confirmed that a few days later. Ginger said she liked me!

On our first date, I got to her house ten minutes early, and she was still wearing her bathrobe and curlers. I had never seen curlers before, except maybe on some woman in a station wagon screaming at her kids. No matter, she still looked good. This was one o'clock in the afternoon. We sat on her couch, drank four bottles of wine, then went over to my place and drank two more. (We still have those empty bottles— along with the other fifty-one bottles of wine we drank together our first year.) It was an amazing, magical day. I ended up taking her home the next morning.

After I dropped her off, I called my buddy Frank to tell him how incredible Ginger was. I couldn't get her out of my mind all day. Everything about her turned me on, including her smell—so clean, so sweet. As we dated, I got a better picture of the whole package: how bright, independent, and caring she was. *And* what a great cook she is . . . She makes hard-boiled eggs just to put in salads. Imagine that.

We were two people who hadn't been looking for a relationship, but we quickly found ourselves on the fast track to the altar. Marriage just seemed like the natural way to consummate our relationship. Why not?

I proposed to her in June, six months after we met. We were married that October.

## ON BENDED KNEE

**Just like the coach said**

In June 1985, we had this glorious trip to Barbados together, and I was all set to propose, but I didn't. I was too nervous. A couple of weeks later, we were back home, dining out one night, and that's when I finally popped the question. My butterflies made me remember when I was a kid, pitching baseball, the coach once asked me if I was nervous, and I admitted that I was. "Good," he said. "That means you care."

# David W.

*Marriage almost blew their relationship*

*"I didn't hear celestial music or see fireworks, but I knew that we belonged together," he says of his relationship with Marlena. David is fifty-three years old, works as a corporate trainer, and enjoys hiking and rock climbing. His marriage to Marlena is his second. They were wed in 1987.*

We were at college. She was a student. I was a teacher. The first time I remember seeing her, she was wearing dungarees and a T-shirt, carrying a load of papers out to her car. It was several years later before it occurred to me to ask her out.

I'm ten years older than her, and that age difference was really a big reservation, for me and for her. She was also worried about the fact that I'd been married before, that I had already been there, done that, and would find everything old hat that she would be experiencing for the first time.

We dated a few months. I was most impressed with how damn smart she was. One day we were standing on a hill overlooking some fields, a place we often went for walks. I was saying something or other, and she interrupted me. "So, shall we just move in together and see how the hell it goes?" I couldn't see any good reason not to.

We lived together for the next seven years. By that time, most everyone we knew thought we were already married. So it seemed like something we should do. In large part, we wanted to marry to make the relationship legal. There are just too many uncertainties when you're not married, and ultimately such things as wills and estates are cleaner when you've got that wedding certificate.

We didn't exactly have a charmed honeymoon. For some time afterwards, we thought that getting married had loused everything up. It was like a door snapping shut. It made us feel claustrophobic. I remember 1987 and 1988 as a stressful time. It took us a long while to learn how to breathe properly. Now that we can, I enjoy marriage. I like the day-to-day continuity of living with somebody who really knows what I'm about.

## REFLECTIONS

### Silence is golden

Honesty has its limits. Some people think that marriage works best when both parties feel free to share anything and everything. But I'm convinced that sometimes it's far better just to shut up and not say everything on your mind. The hurt you may slather onto your spouse with total honesty can take a long, long time to wash off.

# Alan

*A rush to the altar*

*A college professor and clinical psychologist, Alan remained single until he was forty-two. That's when he met Maria, an Episcopal priest, on a blind date. This conversation took place two weeks after the wedding.*

She came out of the house to greet me. She was wearing shorts and a purple top. I remember saying to myself, "Nice." It was noon. We had lunch (pesto), talked, went for a long walk, went to a movie (*Mission: Impossible*), ate dinner, and sat around and talked some more. I didn't leave her till midnight. A day short of three months later, I proposed.

It seemed like we were rushing things, at least to us. We used to say that if either she or I had been acting as therapist or counselor and someone came to us looking for advice on whether to marry, we would certainly have said "give it six more months."

I think we were also both naturally wary, being veterans of the dating scene. I remember Maria saying to me, "Everything about you rings true, so what's the catch?" But we couldn't find a catch. We have compatible interests (neither of us owned a TV, for instance), and similar values (like a deep appreciation for the life of the mind). I was madly in love with her. She was madly in love with me. I was ready for marriage. So was she.

I doubt there will be regrets. I haven't been married long, but so far, it feels awfully good. I like feeling loved, no longer having the hassles of dating, feeling a part of the community in a deeper way, and not feeling "weird" because I'm still single. I like everything about being married—and that includes some great wedding presents!

## ON BENDED KNEE

### Where the air is thin

Maria and I went on a two-week vacation to Montana in August. As part of that trip, we went backpacking and climbed a mountain, 12,542-foot Silver Run Peak, just outside my hometown. At the top, we sang a couple of hymns, ending with "Let All Mortal Flesh Keep Silence." After we finished the first verse, I told her I had come up with a new verse, and I sang my proposal. Ten minutes later, she threw up. Some combination of too much lunch, too sweet a lunch, too much sun, and too much high altitude made her ill. Fortunately, she said yes before she threw up.

# Roger
*Has his mother-in-law to thank*

*He married Gilda in the summer of 1960. He's now in his late fifties, retired, and spending his time enjoying the opera, travel, and reading. He is a former assistant secretary of state.*

I picked her up at her house. It was a blind date. Her sister and my cousin had been friends at Cornell, and that's how I got her telephone number. We were going out for some burgers and to see a movie (something with Doris Day, but I don't remember the name). She was wearing a dress, and she struck me as perky and sweet, likable, and easy to talk to. She had large eyes, a cheerful face, and an athletic figure.

I thought things went real well, although when I called her for a second date, she told me that she couldn't go out with me because she had another date that night. But her mother insisted she ask for a rain check. So, strangely, my mother-in-law is partly responsible for our relationship.

I fell hard for Gilda, could not bear to be apart from her, and, oh, about two years later, asked her to marry me. It was at La Duchesse Anne, a French restaurant in Boston. We had some veal dishes, and I proposed over the dessert wine. Beyond "Will you marry me?" I don't recall what was said. I just remember it as a happy night.

## Larry
*A hush-hush liaison*

> *He worked as an attorney in private practice in New York City for forty-two years. Now retired*

*and living in Florida. He married in 1954, at age twenty-six. He is the author's father.*

A friend of mine told me he had met a girl who looked Oriental, and he knew I liked Oriental-looking girls. (I had spent several years with the army in Korea.) So he set us up on a blind date. I picked her up, we went to see a movie, and in a few hours we were friends. A date or two later, I fell in love.

I wanted to marry her because we seemed to jell so well. She was a true companion, and I liked her smile, her figure, and (my friend was absolutely right) her Oriental-like good looks. In addition, my three best friends all had recently married, and it became very lonely for me.

I proposed on our third date, three or four weeks after we met. I was fearful of telling my mother. She did not think much of my wife's parents, and she wanted me to marry another woman she knew. As a result, Lee and I married secretly in June and waited until October for our formal wedding. Eventually, my mother withdrew her objections, more or less.

## ON BENDED KNEE

### Happy New Year

I took her to a bar-restaurant in a hotel near our houses. It was called the Concourse Plaza and it was,

at the time, the fanciest place in the Bronx. She told me
that she was not certain we would be together on New
Year's Eve, as another man had asked her out. I said,
"You won't go out with him that night because we are
going to marry."

## Gordon
*Seeing through smoke*

> *Brought up in Ottawa, Canada, he met Ilse on*
> *a blind date in September 1952. They were*
> *married the following March. Now in his early*
> *seventies, Gordon, a retired aeronautical*
> *engineer, spends his time with classical music,*
> *acrylic painting, and wood carving.*

Although Ilse struck me as intelligent and articulate,
and she had a nice figure, I wasn't terribly impressed.
She smoked, which did not appeal to me whatsoever.
My father had been a heavy smoker, so I understood
the dangers of smoking from early on.

But I was actively trying to find a mate, had been
for at least a year. I was not enjoying bachelorhood
very much. My work schedule was strenuous, and I
didn't have much time to circulate. I wanted a stable
home life.

As I got to know Ilse, I got to thinking she'd be an asset as a mate. She didn't put on airs. She seemed genuinely interested in me. She was well groomed, highly presentable, and had a great sense of humor. And her mother was attractive and capable, traits that I hoped her daughter would emulate.

One day we were out for a long drive through the countryside and returned at sunset. On the radio, the tune "You Always Hurt the One You Love" was playing, and we were parting with a heavy hug. We were near Montreal, which is really awful in March. I said, "March is a good month to get away on a honeymoon." The next thing I knew, we were officially engaged.

She eventually quit smoking.

## REFLECTIONS

### The importance of in-laws

The in-laws, especially the mother-in-law, should be an important factor in the choice of a bride. There is a high probability that the bride will eventually grow to resemble her mother. Another important issue is the in-laws' degree of marital happiness relative to that of one's own parents. I won't raise the issue of the financial status of the in-laws (mine had little), but I found it desirable to have in-laws who lived with class and civility—regardless of finances. In-laws should have intelligence, and the siblings-in-law should be people you like to spend time with.

# Edward S.
*Never too old*

> *He was married for nearly fifty years to the same woman. She died in 1988. Six months later, he met Sandra at a party in the lobby of the condo where both of them lived. Edward is eighty-three.*

She was wearing a white sweater and white sneakers, and she looked like a college kid. She also resembled my first wife. I had been so lonely. A feeling of hope came over me.

I walked over, a bit nervous, and we chatted. I noticed how beautiful her face was. I asked her to go out to the movies and for a cup of coffee. We went out the next night to see *Driving Miss Daisy*. For six months she dated me but was also seeing another man. I knew him. I said to her what I felt, that he wasn't right for her, that I was. She believed me, and we got married!

She is very intelligent, beautiful, a good friend, and a great cook.

# Steve

*On the way to the forum . . .*

> *He met his future wife on-line, which, he maintains, is the best way to meet a future wife. Steve is forty-seven and writes books about computers. At the time of this interview—which took place on-line—he had been married to Susan for only two months. It was a second marriage for both.*

The first time I saw her was at the Baltimore Washington International Airport. That was our first date. We spent the first two hours or so being driven to our Washington hotel by a childhood friend of mine who has absolutely no sense of direction. When we got to the hotel, we went upstairs and made passionate love for several hours.

At the time we had had an E-mail relationship for several months. She was helping me with my latest technical book, serving as my "official novice," reading the manuscript to make sure that it would be comprehensible to the most computer-illiterate reader. I had put a message on several forums, and a forum participant (I think on Compuserve's Software Development Forum) forwarded it to his brother. The brother forwarded it to Susan because she had said that she wanted to learn how to program.

Anyway, through this process of going back and forth on-line, discussing my book, we fell in love. We were both married at the time, and that was our greatest obstacle to forming a relationship. On Halloween 1995, we were on the telephone. I said, "If we were both single, would you be interested in a personal relationship?" There was silence, and I said, "If that was the wrong question, please ignore it." She said, "No, it was the right question. Yes, I would." And she then was quite insistent that we meet.

When we did, during that trip to Washington, I found her to have all the attributes I wanted in a woman: intelligence, character, attractiveness, and a happy disposition.

## REFLECTIONS

### Electronic liaisons

I think the best way to meet a future spouse is via E-mail. It allows you to get to know him or her as a person before being distracted by physical attractiveness and similar attributes. Those are certainly important but less so than character.

## Rehan
*Finances before fiancée*

> *Born and raised in Pakistan, he moved to the*
> *United States three years ago and now drives*
> *a cab in New York City. He is twenty-three*
> *years old and single but hopes to marry soon.*

Marriage is what everybody does. For tradition's sake, for sex, for children. Yes, of course I want to marry. How can a man be complete without a wife? Just as soon as I have enough money, I'll go back to Pakistan and ask my parents to arrange a marriage for me. I'll have a say in who they choose, but ultimately it will be their choice. That's the way it was for my father, and his father, and his father. I wouldn't consider it any other way.

## Wayne T.
*A good business decision*

> *"I didn't just pop the question out of the clear*
> *blue sky. Being a salesman, I really hate*

*hearing no," he says. "So I felt her out first,
and by the time I finally went for the close, I
was pretty sure that she'd say yes." He and
Jane have been married since 1985. They
have two children. This conversation took
place on a warm spring day at Gino's Pizzeria
near Wayne's bustling real estate office.*

I met her in a bar called Manny's that I used to go to
when I was single. We were introduced, funny enough,
by a close friend of my former girlfriend.

That was 1982. I was thirty. Until then, I hadn't
been ready for marriage. I figured at my age marriage
would soon be followed by kids, and I just couldn't
handle that responsibility. I had this real fear about
being able to provide. By 1982, though, I was just
starting to get in reasonable financial shape. So for the
first time, really, I was at least thinking about getting
married.

I guess settling down appealed to me most because
I couldn't stand the thought of being alone for the rest
of my life. I wanted someone to talk to. And someone
who would be there for me if I ever found myself down
and out. I knew there were some things about being
single, certain freedoms, that I'd be giving up, sure. But
the pros of marriage seemed to outweigh the cons. In
this sense, it was like a good business decision.

So the only question was *who*. Jane and I had become great friends. She also was someone without big expectations of what I could provide materially. I had lots of dates with women whose only concern seemed to be how much money I had at the end of the month. I didn't want someone who would drain me, and there are women who will do that. Jane didn't care how much money I had or made. Hey, but don't get me wrong—I still had her sign a prenuptial agreement!

## ON BENDED KNEE

### A trial run

My father proposed to my mother in front of the Convention Center at Atlantic City, New Jersey. I wanted to do the same. Thought it would make a neat story for the kids. The day before we got to Atlantic City, we were staying in Cape May. That evening, while she was in the hotel, I snuck out and bought a cheapo cubic zirconium ring. I figured I'd give it to her as a deposit, and then we could later pick out a real diamond together. That way, if Jane said no, or if the ring fell into the sand, I'd be out only ten bucks. The next day at the Convention Center, that's when I popped it, just as planned. She said she'd *love* to marry me! Two weeks later, we took the bus into Manhattan down to the Diamond District to shop for a real ring.

# Tom R.

*Fell into a trap*

> *"Marriage seemed like something that would*
> *happen, but I wasn't looking for it," he says.*
> *Tom is thirty-six, owns a picture-frame shop,*
> *and has been married to Sophie since 1991.*
> *They met five years prior to that at a small*
> *party at a mutual friend's house.*

She seemed classy, smart, funny, and attractive. She
had that exotic Jewish look that I've always preferred
to the Waspy blond look. I didn't think I had a shot, so
I didn't even approach her. That would have been that,
but we knew a lot of the same people, so I kept bump-
ing into her in different places. We were at this other
party, and I noticed she had dressed somewhat more
provocatively than usual. She was laying a trap for me.
It worked. All of a sudden, she comes over and asks,
"Do you want to go out together sometime?"

"Yeah," I said to her. "I'd like that." I've never been
one to mind it when a woman comes on strong. I like
it, in fact. There's no guessing game.

We had our first date about a week later—went out
for a casual dinner and a movie. It went well. And so
did every date after that. For a year we dated exclu-
sively. Then for four more years, we shacked up.
That's when I got to thinking that I wanted to elimi-

nate any ambiguity or confusion about our relationship. I wanted to cement the bond . . . to buy things together for us—no longer *your* stuff and *my* stuff, but *our* stuff.

All this was going through my head, but the actual proposal was a spur-of-the-moment thing. I was visiting my parents in Chicago, talking to my mother, complaining about the high cost of wedding rings. I wasn't sure about marriage yet; I was just thinking out loud. Nonetheless, Mom gave me the ring she'd been saving. It had been in the family for a long time and was in perfect condition. I drove home sixteen hours to see Sophie, all ready to pop the question.

When I got home, though, she was really pissed because she had found a videotape a friend made for me of a *Sports Illustrated* swimsuit shoot. She was so mad, and I was exhausted from the drive. I couldn't believe this was happening. So I just showed her the ring to shut her up. She looked at it and said, "This is a wedding ring." I said, "If you want it to be." She lightened up considerably.

## REFLECTIONS

### No free ride

Marriage requires work. You can't get lazy. You've got to listen and share and not hold things back. You've got to have common interests but separate interests, too. Tolerance and respect are a must. And occasional counseling helps. It would improve a number of relationships I know. It could have saved a few marriages of people I've known.

## Bob I.

*Fattened on pasta*

> He describes himself as "vice president of
> development and purchasing and anything
> else they ask me to do." He works for a large
> sporting-goods wholesaler on the West Coast.
> He is forty-one years old. He and Nancy have
> been married since 1979. They have two boys,
> ages eight and ten.

It was in twelfth grade social studies class; she walked into the classroom and into my life. She had just transferred to our school. My first thought was that she looked like Sophia Loren.

For our first date, we went out on my boat to a Memorial Day beach party. I got drunk and scared her out of her mind with my fast and reckless driving. When we returned to shore, she didn't want me even to walk her home. I'd say the whole first year was pretty rocky. Whenever we disagreed on a particular matter or brought up the subject of whether we would continue to date, she would give me her standard line, "Nobody is breaking your arm to date me." The problem was that I was also playing the same game of pretending to be cool. It's a wonder that we stayed together.

About three years later, Nancy's mother proposed to me on Nancy's behalf. I was nineteen. She continued to ask me when I was going to marry her daughter every year until I was twenty-four. In fact, the whole family—the mom and Nancy's sisters (I call them the *she-devils*)—conspired to get me to marry her. They would feed me constantly to fatten me up for the event. They would serve me like a king! I was always suspicious. Then one night, the royal treatment ended. Nancy's mom ripped into me. She started throwing things around, telling me I was taking advantage of her daughter and I should either get married or get out and not come back. I got out that night just in time! (Laughs.)

I figured I'd better marry her. Actually, based upon the qualities that I was seeking in a mate, Nancy had the best fit. She was independent, intelligent, caring, pretty, self-sufficient, frugal, ambitious, extremely capable, family oriented, loved children, and loved me. My only reservation was marrying into that crazy family. I was very concerned about being domineered by those she-devils. Did that ever come to pass? Oh, they're still she-devils, all right, but I've become very adept at hiding from them!

## REFLECTIONS

**Take what you get**

Do not get married to someone with the thought that you are going to change that person. I can guarantee you that it isn't going to happen. People generally do not change that much. They are who they are.

# Caleb
*Marriage the hard way*

> *Married to Rachael when he was twenty, Caleb emigrated from Israel four years later. He is now forty-eight and works as a chauffeur for a limousine service based in northern New Jersey. The couple have three grown children.*

I was young. When you are young, you do stupid things. She got pregnant, so I had to marry her. That's the way it works in Israel. I wouldn't have had much of a life had I not married the mother of my child. The social stigma would have been far too great. Same thing for divorce. You can't do it in Israel. There's great shame in getting divorced. It's not like here. Looking back over the years, I suppose I could have done a lot worse. Rachael isn't too horrible! (Laughs.) It was stupid of me to get her pregnant, but things really haven't worked out so bad.

## Michael M.
*Looking for balance*

> *Two months before this interview, he and his family moved cross-country so that he could take a job as director of public affairs at a Fortune 500 company. His wife, Beth, quit her attorney job to be a full-time mother. The two have been married since 1992. They have a two-year-old son, Maxwell. Michael is thirty-five years old.*

I met her at college when I was eighteen. We were part of the same circle of friends. We dated, broke up, and then started dating again. Numerous times. Why marriage? I don't know. It seemed like the natural progression. Actually, we were about to move in together (while still in college), and her parents strongly suggested that we should only do so if we had the intention of eventually getting married. I guess from that day on, in her parents' living room, we were implicitly engaged.

Things between us haven't been so hot lately. I'm working incredible hours at the new job. I come home wiped, and Beth is often in a bad mood after being alone all day with Maxwell. Then she wants to dump the kid on me. With all this father-sensitivity crap these days, Daddy's supposed to go to work, have his stomach lining eaten out, then come home and play patty-cake until the kid eventually falls asleep at eleven. Then Daddy's supposed to get up at 6:30 in the morning and leave for work again.

Let's not even talk about sex. Beth used to look so hot before we got married. She'd get all dolled up when we'd go out, slip into a black leather miniskirt. What's she going to do now—put on her miniskirt between changing diapers? Even if she did, what would it be for? Maxwell sleeps with her.

I don't want to give the impression that things are all bad. I love Beth and Maxwell dearly. When I came up here to take the job, I came first and lived alone in a hotel room for two weeks. I was glad as hell to have them back. Absence in this case did make the heart grow fonder. I recalled all the reasons I fell for Beth in the first place: her charm, laughter, aura of calm. All I'm saying is that there has to be some balance in life, and I'm having a hard time achieving that right now.

# Jonathan

*Entering another culture*

> *He is forty-two years old, originally from Ohio,*
> *works as a marketing consultant, and enjoys*
> *book collecting, poetry, and gardening. This*
> *conversation took place on the week of his and*
> *Bonnie's first wedding anniversary.*

We were both invited to a Passover seder. I was converting to Judaism and Bonnie was returning to the faith of her parents and grandparents. Wearing a black raincoat, carrying a basket of wine (she is a winemaker), she entered the rabbi's house as one of the last guests. She hugged everyone after she came in. What I remember most distinctly was her smile and her effervescence.

She is a part-time folk singer. Our first date was my going to hear her perform at the local university. She sang about her parents' experiences as Holocaust survivors. Several in the audience were crying. We went out afterward for dinner.

I was three years over getting divorced and was gun-shy about getting involved again. I had dated three women before Bonnie—but found the relationships more about sex than anything else. With Bonnie, it was different. She didn't really fit my ideal body type (I like thinner women), but there was that constant smile and warmth that I just couldn't walk away from. And she was Jewish—and became part of my entering into Jewish life and leaving behind my cold WASP ways.

We had an on-and-off relationship for four years. Then we decided to buy a home together. On one Saturday morning, after we made the purchase but before we moved in, I turned to her on the street outside the house and said, "I guess this means we are getting married." It really wasn't a decision but more like a leap off a cliff.

## REFLECTIONS

**Marriage is work**

It is a constant battle to keep connected intimately and to remember to put our relationship before all the other craziness of modern life. We have taken to scheduling two days a week off that are just for the two of us to spend time together. Like anything of value, I suppose, it takes a lot of time and much effort to make a marriage succeed.

# Ed

*Got himself cornered*

> "My fraternity was having its annual party,
> and the tradition was that everybody find a

*date. So we were all out combing the bars,
looking for someone to ask," he says. "Eva
hung out with a lot of us, and she and I would
talk from time to time. This one night, I'm
talking to her, and a friend walks up to us and
says, 'Ed, why don't you ask Eva to the
party?' I couldn't really say no. I was
cornered." Ed is a soft-spoken man with close-
cropped red hair. He is thirty-two years old
and works as a financial analyst for a large
chemical company. He and Eva were married
in 1990. They have two children.*

I wasn't planning on asking her out. I had never really thought about her romantically. Actually, she got a lot more attractive after we met. In the first six months we were dating, she lost twenty-five pounds. At the same time, we found we had a lot in common, like our taste in clothes, our exercise routines, and our shared sense of right and wrong. We also have the same eating habits. We're not into red meat or sit-down meals; we both like snacking and desserts.

About a year and a half after meeting her, I first started thinking marriage. I had graduated college and got a job; she was still in school. We loved each other. We wanted to stay together. We had been living together. I think like most men in our culture, I was programmed—once I found someone I felt comfortable with, marriage just seemed like the inevitable next step. I spent no time agonizing over whether I wanted to get married or not.

Eva and I kidded around about getting married, which was probably our way of feeling each other out on the subject. By the time I asked her, three years after we met, I fully expected her to say yes. It was at a fancy restaurant, just after our dinner. I pulled out the ring and simultaneously asked her to marry me. She cried, and agreed. We had a big wedding that everyone who attended says was terrific. Lots of drinking. Everybody got up on stage and starting singing with the band.

I don't regret marrying on the young side. I was never a wild swinger anyway. I've been very happy in the role of husband, and I love being a dad.

## REFLECTIONS

**Laissez-faire marriage**

We don't really work on our marriage or even give it a lot of thought. We're just very comfortable with each other. We've been married for seven years. I think if you're working hard on marriage after only seven years, then that's a bad sign—there's probably more trouble to come.

# Joel
*Matrimony in the face of fear*

> *Married to Elana since he was twenty-nine,*
> *Joel, now thirty-five, says he married "to please*
> *her." The couple live in the Pacific Northwest*
> *and have a two-year-old daughter. Joel is the*
> *station manager of an FM radio station.*

I was twenty-five when I met Elana. I was in love. But
I also had this mindset that marriage was like the ulti-
mate entry into middle age, suburban hell, "the estab-
lishment." Let's see . . . (breaking into song) . . . First
comes love, then comes marriage, then comes plaid
polyester pants, ChemLawn, watching "Murder, She
Wrote" reruns, and life membership in the Republican
Party! (Laughs.)

We—she!—started talking marriage after we'd
been together two years. Elana's a couple of years older
than me, and she really felt that old biological clock
ticking away. She wanted to marry, and she made that
very clear! She asked me to explain what I had against
marriage. I told her, but all of a sudden my reasons
sounded silly. So we married.

In truth, there was no way for me to have known
how wonderful marriage would be! And, no, I don't

watch "Murder, She Wrote." My lawn is full of beautiful dandelions. And I voted *twice* for Bill Clinton!

## Tom B.
*Building a false image*

> *Tom, now fifty-four, married Alice when he*
> *was thirty-three. They were divorced two*
> *years later. Tom is the restaurant critic for a*
> *city magazine. He is gay.*

My marriage was an attempt to prove to myself that I was heterosexual. It was also a part of my search for respectability within the community. In those days, there were no models for being openly gay and respectable. I didn't know any way that I could achieve the status I yearned for without getting married. And I wasn't about to join the Kiwanis!

I'm still in touch with Alice; we've remained friends. I have had relationships with numerous men over the past two decades, and at times I think that I'd like to settle down. But marriage? Even if gay marriage became legal in this state, no, I don't think so. I'm not convinced that heterosexual marriage is the best model for gay relationships.

# John B.

## *Strangers in the night*

*Twenty-two years old, a diesel mechanic and recreational bowler, he met Sheila three years ago, while still in high school. Growing up, says John, "I never thought I'd marry. I thought I'd be a loner." Nevertheless, he asked Sheila to marry to him three months after they met. The two are now engaged.*

My friend, Ed, told me that she saw me in school and said she liked me. One night he brought me over to her place to meet her, and we talked on her front stoop for about ten minutes, but it was dark and I couldn't really see what she looked like.

She said the next day she'd be baby-sitting at one of the neighbor's houses, and she gave us the address and told us to stop by. We walked in the door, and she came up and gave me a hug, which I didn't expect. We talked. She told me she liked me but wasn't sure if I liked her. "Yeah," I told her. "I think you're pretty." We started going out regularly after that. I only dated two girls before dating Sheila. But I felt like things with her were going to work out.

Why? She's warm and kind and always on top of things. Like when I need to pay bills, she'll remind me.

We're very honest with each other. And we like a lot of the same things, like camping and keeping a neat, clean house. Personal hygiene is very important to both of us, too.

She envisions having children. I can agree with that, maybe, but many, many years from now. There are a lot of things I want to do in my life before that. It's looking like we may have to negotiate.

## ON BENDED KNEE

### Playing to the crowd

It was at a party at her parents' house, with about forty people there. I got down on my knee, pulled out the ring, and I asked her to marry me. I felt confident she'd say yes, because whatever I did, wherever I went, she wanted to be right there with me. [Sheila walked in and out of the room during this interview, making occasional comments.] When I asked her, her eyes just widened and her mouth dropped, and she said, "Yes." Everybody clapped and cheered.

# Carter

*Into the wild blue yonder*

> *A retired career military man, the colonel is in*
> *his midsixties and spends much of his time*

*golfing, bowling, and playing bridge. He and*
*Libby were married in 1955.*

She was sitting at a college basketball game when I noticed her. Wearing a light sweater with a contrasting colored scarf, she was very pretty, with a magnetic smile. I saw her a few weeks later at the library, and she was just getting up to leave from her study group. I knew one of the other girls at the table, so that was my excuse to wander over. I can't remember exactly what I said, but whatever it was, it worked. Our mutual friend had to take off, and Libby and I went over to the student union for a Coke. We talked for about an hour, and it was like we'd known each other for years.

I had a sense, just a feeling in my gut, that we'd be good partners for life.

I proposed to Libby two months later, and we married three months after that. I was leaving for the air force immediately after graduation, so you might say I was sort of in a hurry. We were sitting on her sorority house porch when I asked her to marry me. Much to my surprise, she said yes.

# 6

# THE CALL TO PROCREATION

## Guys Who Wanted to Be Dads

Some women, particularly those acutely aware of their biological clocks ticking, may sometimes think that they're the only ones who pine for parenthood. But go to the park on a Sunday afternoon. See the faces of the fathers as they watch their daughters riding bicycles for the first time.

Or tell a man that his son looks *just* like him, and watch his eyes light up like he's just won the $10 million jackpot. Mine do when I hear those words (even though I know the person is stretching because Clay resembles his mother quite a bit).

Granted, men's and women's procreation desires do differ. Says Sarah Ossey, M.S.W., C.S.W., psychotherapist, social worker, and president of Providence Matchmaking in New York City, "Women feel the strong need to procreate, to experience childbirth. For men, of course, there's no childbirth experience to be had, except vicariously. And perhaps the need to nurture isn't as strong. But there's still a strong pull to procreate. In a man's case, it has more to do with his own mortality. He yearns to pass on his family name and his image."

There's no law (but perhaps there should be) that two people need to be married to have children. But having Mom and Dad call each other husband and wife sure does make life less confusing. For my good friend Jean-Marc D., a physicist and engineer who spends weekends coaching his son's soccer team, the *main* motivation for marriage was the desire to have kids and to do so in wedlock. "We pretty much got married to legitimize our future children," he says.

For all the married men in this chapter, the dream of raising a family was right up top when they popped the question. As our first entry, Jeffrey, says, "All I ever wanted out of life was to be married and have a family."

# Jeffrey
## *Nibbling his way to marriage*

> *"Lisa had just started a job as the front-desk receptionist at the health club where I worked part time. I looked out and saw her in a tight white shirt leaning across the counter and I noticed her big breasts," says Jeffrey, a graphic designer, martial arts enthusiast, and science-fiction buff in his late twenties. He and Lisa have been married since 1989. They have three children.*

She asked me for a workout routine, so I wrote her one. Later on, while she was at the desk, I snuck behind her and asked her if her boyfriend would mind if I nibbled on her ear. She went, "Uh, uh . . ." and someone came up to the desk and we couldn't talk anymore. A few days later, she put her business card on my car with her phone number and signed it, "Your Saturday Morning Receptionist."

The following weekend, we went out on our first date, to see *Da*, with Martin Sheen. After the movie, we went up to a music studio where she hung out. We met her best friend up there and sang and listened to music. We were there till the wee hours of the morning, and I drove her back to her apartment. Before leaving the car, we talked a bit and I massaged her neck. Then we made out like bandits at the front door and had to push ourselves away. It was great.

That was July. We said our "I love you's" Labor Day weekend and talked marriage. Around November, I applied for and was approved for a consolidation loan that freed up the money I needed to buy the engagement ring. So I told her about the loan and said, "So, you wanna?" I gave the ring to Lisa on Christmas Day.

I always knew I wanted to get married. I always knew I would, too. All I ever wanted out of life was to be married and have a family. Lisa was the right one. That was obvious to me. She made me happier than anyone else in the whole world and I wasn't going to lose her.

## REFLECTIONS

### The sometimes harsh reality

Marriage is never what you expect it to be. It's not Ozzy and Harriet. It's more Dan and Roseanne. There are fights and bad times and long nights and tired nights and sick kids and great sex and no sex and leftovers and money problems and holding each others' heads when you're throwing up from the stomach flu. But you don't want to give it up for anything.

# Arturo

*Where's the ketchup?*

> *Arturo is twenty-eight, repairs ATM machines,*
> *plays soccer, and attends auto races. He*
> *married Carol in 1996, and they have one child.*

I was at the beach. It was July 1994. She was wearing a red bathing suit, looking fine, just gazing out at the ocean. I had to meet her. I walked up, sat down on her blanket, and started talking. To be honest, I don't even remember what I said. She seemed wary but into it. After a few minutes, her girlfriends came back from wherever, so I took off but didn't go too far.

About half an hour later, she stood up. She had a hotter body than I had realized! She was heading for the snack bar, so I figured I'd tag along, take another shot. We talked some more, and she asked me if I wanted a french fry. That was it, that french fry. I knew then we'd be dating. I got her phone number, called her the next day, and we wound up seeing each other like once a week for the next six months or so. A good friend of mine was getting married, and she was my date to the wedding. I thought that would be a good opportunity to ask her to marry me, which I did, right after the ceremony.

Marriage was the thing to do. I didn't have to give it a lot of thought. Carol was pretty, fun to be with, and wanted kids. Also, I feel a man gets more respect when he's married. My only reservation was that her mom has been married three times and her dad's a real loser. That made me a little nervous, thinking maybe because of her family background, she was jinxed.

## REFLECTIONS

**Parallel dreams**

Two people got to have the same dreams. You have a partner with different priorities, and your life can be hell. Say, for instance, one person wants to just hang out all day, and the other expects to live in a huge house, with nice cars and a pool. That is what I'd call a marriage in jeopardy.

# Edward C.
*A case of missing jeans*

> Two years after his first marriage ended in divorce, he met Anne—in the basement laundry room of their apartment building. "She was everything I've always been attracted to in a woman—a petite brunette

*with a pretty face and great body . . . she looked just like Sally Field," he says. That was in 1977, when Edward was thirty. This conversation took place in his office at the successful memorial (tombstone) business that he has owned and operated for the past ten years.*

My first words to her were, "Did you see anyone take off with my jeans?" Someone had apparently taken two pair of jeans from my wash. I wanted to know, honestly, if she knew anything about that, but it was also an excuse to chat her up. She couldn't help me as far as the jeans were concerned, but we did have a nice conversation, and I managed to get her phone number.

Our first date, to dinner a few nights later, didn't go very well. She was newly divorced, and she spent the entire time talking about the breakup. I didn't want to hear it. I felt I had freed up my baggage, and I didn't need anyone else's. But I was physically attracted to her, so I set up a second date, hoping it would go better.

Well, I stood her up. I had a convention to attend in Boston (I was national sales manager with a gift company at the time), and I just forgot that we had the date. I was reminded as soon as I got home. Man, she was pissed—really, really pissed. She called me out on the carpet. I was going out with several girls at the time, so I said to myself, "Who needs this shit?" and I just hung up the phone.

Two months later, she called me and invited me to her apartment for a drink. I went, and I never left! From that point on, I basically lived with her, using my apartment as a place to hang clothes. That was around the end of January; by June, I proposed. We had gone to the Jersey shore together, where I was attending a business show. That's where I asked her to marry me. I think she probably would have wanted to date some more before getting hitched again—but I was too good a catch for her to lose!

For me, on the other hand, the timing was just right. I wanted kids, and Anne said she did, too. [Points to the photos on his desk of his teenage son and daughter.] And Anne was pretty, smart, educated, from a good family, and had a sense of humor. I was also driven to achieve business success, which was something she understood and appreciated, something my first wife never did.

## REFLECTIONS

**We are products of our upbringing**

I think it was inevitable that I married the first time, and that when that didn't work out, that I married again. I feel comfortable being married. It's what I'm used to and what I always saw for myself. When I was a kid, my parents and all my uncles and aunts would get together at different functions. I think we all kind of emulate our parents and our parents' lifestyles, at least to a degree. Marriage is a part of that emulation.


# Martin
*She fit into his dreams*

> *He is seventy-two years old, a retired*
> *attorney. He grew up poor, from a broken*
> *family. His father left home when he was*
> *twelve. He met Jackie when he was sixteen*
> *and she was fourteen.*

There were these benches along Kings Highway (Brooklyn)—kind of like on the Champs Élysées in Paris, but not as elegant—where all the kids would hang out. I was with a group of my friends, and she was with a group of hers when we met. She was wearing a short skirt, loose-fitting blouse, and a baseball-type jacket. She had *class* written all over her. She was a hothouse flower in the ghetto where we lived. I loved her from the moment I saw her.

We had our first date about a week later. We walked along Kings Highway, people-watching, talking about our dreams for the future. Me, I told her about wanting to get an education, leaving the ghetto, and making a career.

Jackie was the antithesis of everything I'd ever known. She was from a stable, loving family, where they never yelled at each other. In our family, yelling was an art form. She had all that I wanted . . . elegance, beauty, maturity. I wanted to do things right in my life, to be all the things my father was not—a good husband and father, for example. Jackie fit right into the picture.

Two years after we met, I joined the Army Air Corps. By then, we knew we would marry. I would do all the talking about it, and I took her silence as consent. No proposal was necessary. I sent her money out of my army pay. She saved it in a separate account. If we changed our minds, she would have returned the money. But that never happened. I wasn't going to let such a good thing get away.

# Richard
## *To friendship and beyond*

*He's in his midthirties, works as a freelance magazine writer, and enjoys hiking, mountain biking, and spending time with his and*

*Rachelle's two children. They married in 1986.*
*Part of why he married, says Richard, "I loved*
*her kisses."*

We got together in college. I was a senior, the newspaper's editor, and she was associate editor. I met with her in late summer to discuss the upcoming year. She was wearing a purple top that dipped in a *V* to about midsternum. She was tan and attractive. When I dropped her off, it felt like a date, but it wasn't. We didn't kiss until she left the paper after the first quarter. I suppose we were both overwhelmed with too many activities. Plus, she found me too demanding. I said, "Maybe now we can be friends." We finally got mildly drunk together one night and wound up in each other's arms. I remember thinking before I kissed her, "If you do this, Richard, you might be in it for a long time."

We graduated and she went to Massachusetts. I returned to Fargo [North Dakota], where I grew up. We talked a lot on the phone, but it all seemed pretty hopeless. Then I moved to the New York area, and we started seeing each other on weekends, driving four hours each way. Finally, she looked for work in the New York area and got an offer. But she didn't want to move unless she knew we were a going thing. After much agonizing, it seemed obvious that we were destined to be together. We joke that we didn't have a romance—we had a history. It just seemed like we couldn't escape each other. We were engaged for a year and a half, something like that, before we married. I had always figured I'd get married around age twenty-five, and that's when I did.

What made me decide to marry Rachelle? We see eye-to-eye on a lot of things. We both come from strongly religious families (though from very different traditions) and share many values; I knew we would someday be able to raise a family well together. She is intelligent, has a quick—even caustic—wit, and a wonderful laugh. She really takes care of herself without being vain. (This is a very difficult-to-find combination of traits.) Physically, there was no awkwardness between us. We just seemed to mesh.

I don't know what I'd do without Rachelle. Hoo-boy. Sometimes I think I'd make a hell of a priest. If I ever had to date another woman, I'd be just like Woody Allen in the lobster scene of *Annie Hall*, with a woman who is not Annie.

## ON BENDED KNEE

**A free dessert**

I took her to the Charthouse restaurant on the banks of the Hudson in Dobbs Ferry [New York]. We were seated more or less in the middle of the room, so I felt a bit self-conscious, being furtive with the ring and all. Toward the end of dinner, she got up for something, probably the bathroom, and when she came back, I was prepared and gave her the ring. She immediately showed her ring to the waitress and hit her up for free dessert.

# Yong-Kwan
*Marriage, Korean style*

> *He came to the United States to study but returned to his native South Korea in 1978, at age twenty-nine, to find a bride. "My parents thought I should marry before I turned thirty, and I had a strong desire to raise a family," he says. Yong-Kwan found Hyeryung and took her back to America to start his engineering career. They have a grown son and a teenage daughter and live in New Jersey. Because many Americans find "Hyeryung" difficult to pronounce, she goes by the name "Heddy."*

By Korean standards, we had a contemporary marriage, not a real traditional one. I call it a "modified arranged" marriage. My younger brother knew Heddy's younger brother, and they suggested we meet. I asked about her background, family, and education, and she seemed to fit the profile of what I was looking for in a wife, so I asked to be introduced.

We got together in a teahouse, accompanied by our brothers, who stayed with us for about fifteen minutes and then left. Heddy and I talked and walked for two or three hours. I felt right away that she was the right girl. For one thing, she was tall (5'3"), and I wanted a tall wife. I always tended to like tall girls. Consciously or unconsciously, I'm not sure, this may have had to do with genetics. I'm short (5'2"), and I wanted my sons to be taller. Tall boys have an advantage in life.

After the meeting, I told my brother I liked Heddy, but we needed someone to introduce the families. We asked a professor of mine from college. Professors in Korea are very much respected. All the parents would have to agree before we married. At my age, nearly thirty, it was almost a formality—not hard for me to convince them! But Heddy was only twenty-three, so it was much more difficult with her parents. For one thing, I had been living in the States, so there was no way for them to know that I wasn't some kind of wild playboy!

We married within several months of meeting and returned to the States. The first two years didn't work out so well. She had expected me to be soft and cute; she found out I was a much stronger person. But we had a commitment to work things out, and after two years, we started to find our way.

## PLANNED PARENTHOOD

### Children of good stock

I felt my wife should be Korean. I felt my children should be Korean. If I had married an American girl, the children would have been of mixed race, and I wasn't ready in my twenties to accept that. But that was then. I'd spent most of my life in Korea, and I was very much more Koreanish than I am now. If I were marrying today, it might be different.


# Jeremiah
## *Joining the family*

> *A thirty-six-year-old staff sergeant in the U.S. Marine Corps, he married Audrey in 1995. It was the second time around for both of them. "My first marriage, when I was nineteen, was to the first girl I ever dated. I married her because I always wanted to get married and have a family. But I was too young to know what to look for in a wife," he says.*

I met her at the club on base for staff NCOS. On some days, they let civilians in. A lot of girls come there just looking to party, have a good time, maybe find some guy with money. Audrey looked different, more mature, professional, like someone who wanted to make a good life for herself. She was also attractive, not overweight, and even though she's almost seven years older than me, she looked young. I was separated and hoping for a new relationship.

We talked for awhile, but I didn't get her number. Luckily, my buddy got her friend's number, so we wound up double-dating a few times before I took her out alone. About a year after we started dating (during which time I divorced my prior wife), Audrey and I moved in together. By that time, I was already thinking marriage, but what really made up my mind was meeting Audrey's family. She's from a family of twelve, and I found them great. I always wanted to be part of a big family. Of course, that wasn't the only reason I wanted to marry her. We made excellent partners around the house—like when the house needs cleaning, we do it together. When she cooks, I do the dishes. When I cook, she does the dishes.

We also have very similar values, both raised in the church. When we first started going out, for instance, it was something like six months before we did anything. I knew she wasn't going to be fooling around with just any guy. I respected that. We also have similar ideas about how to make marriage work, like talking things out when we're angry at each other. And we know that we need to spend time together but that we also need time for her to go out with her girlfriends and for me to go out with my guy friends.

## REFLECTIONS

### Marriage isn't for sissies

Any marriage is going to have its ups and downs, and there will be times that you'll be really angry at the other person. But you can't stay mad. You got to talk about your problems. I can't go to work when I'm mad at Audrey. If I leave the house feeling angry, I'll wind up turning around and coming back. That's hard, but there's no other way. You got to talk.

# Jean-Marc D.

## *For the sake of the children*

*He met Marie-Helene picking grapes in the south of their native France. It was 1979. The two were on summer break from college. When he graduated a year later, he moved to California, and she followed a year after that.*

*They decided to stay in the United States,*
*earn advanced degrees, marry, and start a*
*family. Jean-Marc is forty-four and works as a*
*physicist and engineer for a large*
*telecommunications company. Marie-Helene*
*teaches college French. They have two*
*children, Laurent (thirteen), and Camille (six).*

You arrive at the vineyard, you meet everybody else, and then for the next couple of weeks, you work the fields, eat, and sleep with those people. Marie-Helene and I were in a group of six or seven. We took to each other, and after the day was over, we'd walk along the country roads. This was where, on one dark night, we first kissed.

I was twenty-six and certainly didn't have marriage or children in mind. I think I was like many of my generation. Why marry? Why have kids? I grew up thinking the world was going to go up in a huge radioactive cloud anyway.

Time, I guess, and maybe moving to upbeat California, drove away my pessimism. Marie-Helene and I were living together and started to talk about having kids. Yeah, children came up first, before we discussed marriage. We pretty much got married to legitimize our future children—that was a big rationale for both of us. It also would have upset her parents terribly had we not married.

We went back to France for the wedding, to Marie-Helene's village. We got married in the town hall, not in the church. That was hard for the older generation, but it's what we wanted—a great, big pagan feast of a wedding. No one had cars; all seventy of us walked a mile from her parents' farm to the village. Then we all walked back, stopping at three bars for drinks along the way!

## REFLECTIONS

### Matrimony in America

You meet men in this country who have been married three or four times. In mainstream America, that's how a man can have multiple women, often successively younger women, and keep his respectability. If he simply shacked with up with them, he'd be called a "womanizer." But if he marries each one he sleeps with, well then that's perfectly okay. The community doesn't look down on that.

# Scott B.
*Succumbing to a desirable destiny*

> *"I'd seen her interact with kids, and it almost brought tears to my eyes. I thought from a nurturing standpoint, for myself and any*

*future children we might have, I couldn't have asked for better than Beth Ann," he says. They met in 1986 and married in 1989. Scott, who stands 6'4", is a certified public accountant, an avid weight lifter, history buff, and coin collector. He is now thirty-three years old; Beth Ann is twenty-nine. They had a son in 1993 and twin girls in 1996.*

I always thought of marriage as part of the natural progression of things . . . you go to college, get a job, find a wife, have kids. All that said, when I met Beth Ann, I was a young guy, and much more into the size of my arms and my bench press (then 345 pounds) than I was into women.

We met through my buddy Jim, who was dating Beth Ann's college roommate. Our first night out, we were part of a foursome. I was impressed with how nice and sweet she was. We were sitting on her roommate's bed at 2:00 in the morning when I leaned over to kiss her, and she didn't push me away.

The next night, I just showed up at her dorm room without calling, and she was really turned off by that. I apologized by sending her a dozen red roses, and she decided to give me another chance. We started to see each other regularly. I was head over heels in love, and already fantasizing about marrying her.

The others girls I'd dated were moody. Beth Ann was always very, very even. I grew up in a stressful household where there was a lot of criticism and quibbling. I didn't want that. And with Beth Ann, I knew I wouldn't get it. These days, I see so many guys coming home to women who bust their stones for one thing or the other. Beth Ann never does.

I also see other men who are devalued by their wives. I know one woman who runs around town telling people what a loser her husband is! Imagine. Financially, I've done all right for myself, but that doesn't matter so much. Beth Ann loves me for who I am. She accepts me. That's so important. I wanted to grow old with someone I wouldn't have to impress, who wouldn't put lofty expectations on me.

She's also someone I can have fun with, and she appreciates my interests. For example, I know deep down Beth Ann doesn't give a rat's ass about my coin collection, but when I get excited and have a story to tell about it, she listens. And she takes pride and joy in my accomplishments, just as I do in hers.

## ON BENDED KNEE

### Banking on the future

We'd been talking about marriage, and both sets of parents had been pushing us to get married, but nothing was final. In August 1988, we were up with her parents in Essex, Connecticut, at a jazz festival, when suddenly I heard her mother go "Agggghhhhh." I thought maybe she had heatstroke. No. Beth Ann had just asked her if she could make a wedding for us in a year. My future mother-in-law was ecstatic. We went back to Beth Ann's parents' house and talked plans. That Monday morning we drove down to the bank, where I had my safe-deposit box. I'd already bought the ring. I took it out, put Beth Ann's hand in mine, and said, "I love you. Do you want to spend the rest of your life with me?"

# 7

# IN SEARCH OF PURPOSE

*Men on a Mission*

These guys didn't marry on the spur of the moment. And they had greater things in mind than simply finding a playmate. They married to be with someone for life, someone who could make them feel whole, or assist in their personal growth, or give them a reason for being.

Says relationships guru John Gray: "Men marry in large part to find purpose. Women give meaning to a man's life. A man goes out into the world and sweats and toils, but at some point begins to wonder what it's all for. That's where marriage comes in. A wife is someone who can share in the rewards of his life. She can give a man purpose, a meaning in his life."

Steve P., thirty-six, editor at a national men's magazine, put it to me this way: "I like the fact that my priorities are set. Making decisions is easier for me when I just keep reminding myself that the most important thing in my life is my marriage—more than the job or anything else. And it's comforting that I'll always know where my home is. It's wherever *she* is."

In this chapter you'll meet Keith, who says that Wendy "made me feel important, like I was it." And you'll meet Bill, who says of Leah, "[She] brings out the best in me." And according to Greg W., the first man presented in this chapter, Celeste is someone who helps him grow closer to God.

## Greg W.

*Aided by cannon fire*

> *A thirty-two-year-old native Kansan, he met his wife, Celeste, in 1987 while they were still in college. The two were married in October 1988. Greg is currently a stay-at-home dad with three kids but says he is looking for work in bookkeeping or construction. He reads*

*Christian fiction and* Star Wars *books, surfs the Net, and follows professional and college sports.*

Celeste and I were going to Campus Christians, and for a good while we only talked briefly. She didn't even know that I was interested in her until I asked her to a football game. It was our college homecoming. This was Kansas, and it was October and plenty cold. We had blankets that we put around us, and at some time during the game I started holding her hand. Also, every time our side scored a cannon blasted, and Celeste (who never did like loud noises) would cringe against me.

Nine months later, I proposed. I'd always known I'd get married someday. I wanted someone to take care of me, someone I could feel comfortable around, someone to accept me as I am and to help me grow closer to God. Celeste seemed like the right one. She was the first lady I had dated that I could sit down with and just talk to about anything.

After a four-month engagement, we married. The marriage has seen ups and downs, but it is very rewarding to work through all of the inevitable problems that come up between two people. It is also rewarding to work together with someone to overcome the problems that life dishes out.

## ON BENDED KNEE

### Cub Scout

She was living in Tulsa, Oklahoma, at the time, and I was in Chanute, Kansas. I drove down there one morning and woke her up by ringing the bell. I was standing at her front door with a bear puppet that had a note in its front paws that said, "Greg would like to know if you will marry him." I didn't say a word. She read the note, whispered her answer in the bear's ear, and then went back to sleep. I stayed at her apartment and waited. She awoke midmorning and asked me if I got the answer from the bear. I told her that the bear wanted me to hear it directly from her. So she nodded her head and said, "Yes."

# Dan B.

*Drawn to her toothy smile*

*Like many young Americans in the 1970s, he frequented discotheques. That's where he met Lisa. "I went over to her with absolutely the stupidest line in the world. It's amazing she didn't slug me," he says. Dan is a dentist and a fanatic about golf. Lisa is a marriage therapist with an office next to Dan's. They met and married in 1977. He is forty-five years old. The couple have a seventeen-year-old girl and a sixteen-year-old boy.*

I was in dental school, and one of my class chums and I were going out for the night, and we wound up in this disco. "You see that girl over there," he said to me, pointing to Lisa. "I'll bet those are caps on her front teeth." So I walked over, and I explained that I was a dental student, and I asked her if her front teeth were capped.

They were.

We spoke briefly and a few nights later had our first date. We went for dinner at this restaurant called the Pleasant Peasant and then to see *All The President's Men*. We enjoyed each other's company a lot. There was definite chemistry. I fell in love with her that night.

I hadn't given a lot of thought to getting a wife, and I didn't really have any height, weight, or hair-color requirements. The only thing I knew was that the woman I would marry would have a sense of humor. Lisa certainly had that. She'd respond to my little quips, laughing, but not in a stupid way. She was always upbeat and made me feel good. She was also sensitive, creative, and generous.

We had only been dating a few months, and one night we were out for dinner, and I just found myself proposing. It surprised even me. (Laughs.) I told her that I was getting out of school in four or five months and asked what she thought would happen to our relationship. (I was planning to leave Atlanta.)

"What are you offering me?" Lisa said.

And I said, "Do you want to marry me?"

## LOVE STORY

### A driving force in the relationship

It takes a lot to faze Lisa. One time she was driving around the perimeter highway around Atlanta, and she missed her exit. Instead of figuring out how to turn back, she just drove around the whole loop—about fifty miles—figuring she'd get to where she needed to go, eventually. She's like that, much more laid-back than I am. I would have said, "Damn it," got all uptight, and spun the car around looking to make up for lost time. We complement each other well.

# Keith

*She made him feel important*

*Thirty-five years old, a large man with a soft voice, he supervises an assembly line at a car-battery factory. His interests include hunting and NASCAR races. He was introduced to Wendy*

*by a mutual friend in 1986, at a fund-raiser
for the local volunteer fire department. The
two were married a year later. They have two
boys, ages three and eight.*

I had just gone through a three-year relationship, and I wasn't looking for another relationship at the time, although I think I was always into the idea of getting married. But we started dating, and then I wound up proposing to her five months later. It was a lot of things—her bubbly personality, the fact that she was a good friend, and the notes she'd write me.

Wendy sent me a card every couple of days from the time we met to the day we married. She'd tell me her feelings about me, like no one had before. That was really important to me. It made me feel important, like I was it.

I guess the way she thought about things had a lot to do with it, too. Like she had this one friend who was messing around on her boyfriend. And even though Wendy didn't like the boyfriend, she was really upset by what her friend was doing and started to distance herself from her. That really impressed me. I never wanted to be cheated on. That's one of my biggest fears, and I didn't want to ever have to worry about it. I figured with someone who felt that strongly, as Wendy did, it would never happen to me.

## A WEDDING TALE

**A moment of panic**

Maybe five minutes before the service, I realized that I left the rings at home. So I went storming out of the church, grabbed someone's keys, and tore out of the parking lot. Well, I didn't have time to explain this to Wendy, so when she saw me bolt, she thought that I was running out for good! She was kind of nervous to begin with that day, but at this point, she really started to panic. Luckily, I didn't have far to go, and I was back in no time!

# Mel

*Creating a new beat*

> *Former newspaperman turned college history professor, he married Alma in 1956, a year after they met.*

I was a brand-new reporter for the *Hartford Courant*, doing a series on the city slums. Alma had just started work as secretary to the chief health inspector. When I first walked into the office, she was wearing a short-sleeved blouse and a plaid skirt. I wanted to ask her out right away, but I was too shy. So after the interviews were over, I came up with this idea to create a health department "beat" so that I'd have an excuse to keep on seeing her. It worked.

I was attracted mostly to her great brown eyes, but her big tush didn't hurt either! We talked over the weeks and months, and I found her incredibly sweet and down-to-earth. Finally, after about four months of seeing her at her office and getting to be buddies, she told me she had a friend who might like to go out with me. I said, "How about you?" We went to dinner and had a great time. Two months later, I asked her to marry me.

At that point I was twenty-five and had dated long enough. I had come from a broken home, and I very much wanted to have a loving family life. The romantic, domestic imagery offered to college grads of 1952 made great sense to me. A loving partner to share life with, to have adventures with, to raise children with—that's what the good life was all about.

## REFLECTIONS

### Commitment, commitment, commitment

Love is built by hard work, sharing and caring, fighting like crazy at times, achieving big and little triumphs, and sometimes getting beaten up by life. After forty-one years, you will really know what love is all about. Unless you've made a dreadful mistake in your choice of partners (in which case get out before there are children!), don't even think about divorce. Think about how to make the marriage work. Think about growing old and whether you want to do it alone or with someone you love.

## Greg S.
*He won her away from the other guy*

> *"We went to play Frisbee in the park. She was late and a terrible Frisbee player. We finally sat down on the curb next to my car and started talking. We talked for six hours nonstop. It was absolutely glorious," says Greg of his first date with Sheri. He is forty-one years old, the finance director of a nonprofit public interest group. The curbside chat took place in 1979, shortly after he met Sheri at a meeting to organize a community event. The two married in 1984.*

When I saw her the first time, she was wearing a brown sundress and spoke very confidently with good ideas and opinions. I couldn't wait to bump into her again at the next organizing meeting. I even brought my brother along just so I could point her out!

I had to ask her out several times to get her to date me. After that, she warmed up to me quickly. After we had dated two months, she revealed that she was already engaged to someone else, but she loved me. Teary eyed, she walked out to try to make it work with him, but she came back a couple of weeks later, deeply apologetic, and said she only wanted to be with me.

We dated for another four years. I knew she wanted to marry, but I wasn't ready. Then, one night, I can vividly remember sitting at my desk at home, being suddenly and profoundly struck with the realization that I *had* to make sure she would *always* be in my life. It wasn't so much a calculated decision, but rather a discovery about myself. I wanted her as my lifelong mate.

Why? She's beautiful, extremely smart, self-confident, she laughs so easily, and she's *unbelievably* attentive to me. I love having the attention and respect of someone who knows me better than anyone else—including myself!

## ON BENDED KNEE

### Under the Mexican sky

We were vacationing in Guadalajara, riding in a horse-drawn carriage. It was dusk. I planned to pop the question, but I was thwarted by the driver, an old man who suddenly decided that he would give us a narrated tour—in Spanish. It took a few ungrammatical attempts, and I'm afraid I hurt his feelings, but I finally got him quiet. As we entered a path under giant trees in a gorgeous park, I jumped to the facing seat in the carriage, dropped to one knee, pulled a ring out of my pocket, and asked, "Will you marry me?" I had to ask three times before I could get an answer, she was so stunned!

# Jim

*A surprise after twenty-five years*

> *He met his future wife when he was eighteen, and she was fifteen. "Although she lied," he says. "She told me she was sixteen— something I didn't find out about till our twenty-fifth anniversary!" Jim and Jane were married in 1957. He is now sixty-four years old, recently retired, and living in Florida.*

I was on summer vacation, working as a camp counselor in New Hampshire. She was an apprentice in summer stock. I met her on a multiple blind date. Unfortunately, she wasn't my date. I liked her right away, and I tried unsuccessfully to get her to switch. At a party a few weeks later, I ran into her again. We spent the whole evening together dancing and talking, then went outside, sat under the stars, and necked. I think I knew right then that I wanted to spend the rest of my life with her.

She was so sweet and innocent. There was nothing phony about her—except that she lied about her age, and I forgive her this one flaw. There were no "hard to get" tricks, although she wouldn't go "all the way" until we were married. I was mad about that, and at one point I said good-bye, but I quickly returned because I loved her.

## REFLECTIONS

### Selflessness is key

Our marriage over the past forty-one years has been unique. You could literally count our fights on one hand. We care more for each other than we care for ourselves. That selflessness, I believe, is the most important element in a successful marriage.

# Wayne M.
## *The devil made him do it*

> *He plays bass guitar in an alternative rock group and is also working part-time toward his college degree in human resources management. He met Kim when he was*

*twenty-five. They were at a backstage party given by a mutual musician friend. It was Halloween night. The couple married a year later, in 1989; they have two boys.*

She was wearing a devil's costume—horns, pitchfork, all that—done in a very provocative way: low cut and tight. When I saw her, I was heading out the door with a woman I had just met, and I stopped in my tracks. Kim gave me this alluring look that needed to be answered.

I ditched the woman I was with, and I walked over to Kim with the basic icebreaker, "Hey, how you doing?" We started talking, and it was as if the whole room around us became opaque, like she and I were in our own separate reality. I was totally fixated on her. We walked out toward our cars, and I noticed she was pretty intoxicated, so I decided to drive home with her. There we were, swerving through the streets, her driving, but my hand reaching across to grab the wheel. It was fun. The next thing I remember, I'm waking up in her bed.

At this point in my life, I viewed marriage as staunch, stuffy, and prisonish. It represented the great social squelch—the sooner you succumbed, the sooner you lapsed into convention, the sooner you lost your identity. But after a month with Kim, I started to feel differently. I wanted her to know I was by her side, always. The way you tell someone that in our society is to marry. I guess we could have been this hippie couple, living together for decades, having kids, never marrying. That sounds cool. But I don't know how many are really big and bold enough to do it. I believe that those who do it without the paper are stronger. The legal marriage is a kind of crutch.

## A MARRIAGE TALE

### A private affair

No limos, no room at the Hilton, no tuxedos, no rice. We just ran off to a justice of the peace and got married. I love the fact that our marriage wasn't laced with traditional stuff. I see a big wedding as something you do for others. We were two little gluttonous pigs, running off doing something just for ourselves! Her mom wasn't happy about that. When we told her, she looked me in the eye angrily and said, "I'll never forgive you for this." She has yet to take that back.

# Dan P.

*Acted in spite of his friends*

> *"Before I got married, my buddies would say to me, 'Marriage sucks. It's like prison without bars.' Now, looking back in retrospect, I think*

*they were just joshing," he says. Dan is*
*twenty-eight years old, drives an 18-wheeler,*
*and is a volunteer firefighter. At the time of*
*this interview, he and Lisa had been married*
*for one year, and she was six-months pregnant*
*with their first child.*

First time I saw her was at the supermarket where we were working. I was twenty-four, working as a stock clerk. Lisa was the office manager. She was sitting at her desk, wearing a red smock (the official business uniform), and black jeans. Damn, I thought, she's awfully cute.

Every day at work, I'd talk to her. But I don't think we got along too well. I was rude, cocky, and obnoxious. That was my nature. I'd just gotten out of the army, and I still had the attitude they teach you there. And I was a pretty messed-up individual at twenty-four.

After a year of working with her, I made her ask me out. I said to her one day, "Hey, when you gonna take me out and get me drunk?" And I gave her a little piece of paper with my phone number on it. She just looked at me as if she was thinking I was nuts. But two days later, she called. We dated for something like six months, and then I started thinking marriage, which I had never done before.

She was the one I wanted, though. She was the one I wanted to spend the rest of my life with. I had absolutely no reservations about that whatsoever. She's wonderful . . . sexy, funny, wants kids. And she's very interested in what I do, like fire fighting. I sometimes think she's more interested in that than I am! (Laughs.) I wouldn't trade Lisa for the world.

## ON BENDED KNEE

**A written invitation**

Because I'm not very good with words, I went to the mall to get one of those create-a-cards they have at Hallmark. She likes Garfield (the cartoon cat), so I made one up with Garfield that said a bunch of stuff, I don't remember it all, but it ended with the words, "Will you marry me?" I took her out to dinner, and while she was eating her dinner, I slipped her the card. As she was reading it, I held out the ring across the table. She looked up and started crying, and then she said, "Yes." But she didn't even have to—the answer was pretty obvious.

# Jean-Marc L.

*A Parisian love story*

> *Twenty-five years old, raised in Canada and France, a management consultant, he married*

*Cecile in September 1997. They live in Paris.*
*This conversation took place on-line.*

We were eighteen, just starting college. We were in the same class and simply said "bonjour" to each other. I thought she was real nice and very attractive. Then I learned she had a boyfriend, and I was disappointed. I also had a girlfriend at this time. It was only later, when we both left our respective friends, that I began the famous French process called *faire la cour* (to court a woman). At first, she was not interested, or at least did her darnedest not to seem interested, so it was really slow going.

But she was intelligent, from a friendly family, Catholic, and very beautiful—for all these reasons, it was worth my trouble to pursue her. I'd always thought I would get married someday, to have someone to care for, someone to share everything with, someone to completely trust. Cecile was a good candidate.

After we had been dating for four years, I asked her to marry me. We had a nice evening together, a quiet dinner and a drive in my car, and I proposed just before she got out to go home. (Kneeling isn't really part of the French tradition as it is in Anglo culture, so the car was just fine!) She asked for some time to think about my proposal, took two days, and then when I saw her again, she agreed to marry me!

# John R.

## *A trip to the Falls*

*"Some people move around the planet trying to find happiness; others follow a comet; I thought I would find happiness in marriage,"* he says. John, fifty, is a teacher by trade, now working with recovering adolescent drug addicts and alcoholics in a residential treatment facility. His hobbies include woodworking and canoeing. He and Sallie have been married since 1967.

Our first date was to see the movie *The Endless Summer*, after which we drove from Lansing, Michigan, to Buffalo, New York. Drove through the night. After the movie I had asked her where else she would like to go, and Sallie said, "Niagara Falls." Sure! Took her to her apartment to get some things and we left. I thought we were off to share a romantic weekend. When we got halfway there, she asked if I would like to visit her folks in Buffalo. Ha. Once again, brains triumph over lust! We spent a nice, innocent Saturday and Sunday with her parents.

Our second date was to Chicago to see my brother and sister-in-law. Once there, my sister-in-law, who thought I should have been already married, proposed for me by asking me if I was going to marry Sallie. I said, "Of course." This was after a long night of barhopping in Chicago, but my sister-in-law was cold-stone sober when she popped the question. The next night I called Sallie's parents and asked for their daughter's hand.

It all happened very quickly. After we had been married for about fifteen years, we discovered that we had both decided to call off the engagement and had arranged to meet at a drugstore soda bar to tell the other that the deal was off. But once there, each of us was too chicken to follow through. So we got married by default. Well, that wasn't the only reason! I married Sallie because she is very intelligent, can argue really well, tells the truth, is a Democrat, is very attractive, and does what she says she is going to do.

Our marriage has been hard work and has grown with us—or perhaps in spite of us. Not at a steady, gentle pace, but by fits and starts, leaps and bounds. Sometimes it almost comes apart; then, one or the other of us does some growing, and it holds together.

## AT FIRST GLANCE

### Quite an entrance

I first became aware of this statuesque blond person in an 8:00 A.M. radio production class at Michigan

State University. It was the fall semester of 1966. She was late to almost every class, and her entrance usually caused the teacher to pause and stare. He was too chicken to say anything to her. Quite an entrance. Looked practiced. Like the star walking onto the set. It got my attention.

# Rick

## *Finding his compass*

> *"All of the men in my family have had the good fortune to marry exceptional women. We bumble along, distracted and daydreaming, while the women make sure we don't lose the trail," he says. Rick is fifty, runs a family owned clothing-store chain, plays bass guitar in a country-and-western trio, and pilots a hot-air balloon. He and Julie married in 1985. It was a second marriage for both.*

We live in a small town. I had seen her around, this real fox. She got a job at the local radio station and started selling me advertising time. We talked about a lot of things besides ads. Her marriage was not in good shape, and I think she appreciated a sympathetic ear. I was doing some acting back then, and so was Julie, and we wound up in the same play together, *Tomb with a View*. I don't remember much about it—only that I died. Stabbed in the back. One night after my tremendous death scene, Julie and I went out for coffee, and then she came home with me.

I really fell for her. She had wisdom, common sense, a good business head, the ability to stay focused, a cute face, and great legs! All the same, I had no burning desire to get married. In fact, I'd been single for about seven years, and I found it kind of a hoot. Julie didn't give me any ultimatum or anything, but after a couple of months I could tell she was unhappy that the relationship wasn't progressing. She didn't like the idea of these two divorced people having a decades-long affair. So I proposed. What the heck.

## A WEDDING TALE

### Stuck in Rio

We decided it would be cool to get married in Rio. So we ran away—or *tried* to run away—without anyone knowing. But a nurse spilled the beans while we were gone: "That nice Jones boy was in for blood tests. He and some girl are running away to Brazil to get married." So when we got home, everyone was expecting an announcement, and they were confused when we didn't say anything. Well, that's because we never got married in Rio. Evidently, in Brazil there are so many multiple marriages that it's law you must at least warn your present spouse by publishing an announcement in the paper thirty days ahead of time. Nobody at the Brazilian consulate told us this. Two weeks after we got back, we had a small gathering at a local campground, immediate family only.

# Bill
*He changed his opinion*

> *Now in his early thirties, he knew Leah since the fourth grade. In high school, they were part of the same clique. "But I didn't particularly like her. I actually thought she was rather abrasive," says Bill. When he bumped into her on the street six years later, however, his feelings changed. The two began a relationship that, four years later, led them to exchange vows. Bill teaches education at an East Coast college. At the time of this interview, he and Leah had one child, with another on the way.*

I ran into Leah just as my last marriage was dissolving. My first wife and I were going away on vacation to figure out whether we should stay together or split up. (And we decided to split.) I was taking my ex-wife's dog—an annoying little twit of a dog—over to my mother's house. Anyway, Leah was with her mom, who saw the dog and said something like, "Oh, look at the cute puppy." Leah looked over at the little twit, then at me, and we recognized each other.

We decided to get together, went out to a museum and for some coffee. That started a relationship, sort of, that lasted about three years. We saw each other from time to time, with just an occasional good-night kiss. It was right out of *When Harry Met Sally* . . . . For me, the whole thing was kind of weird, seeing this person I used to hang around with in high school. I was also still coming off my divorce, and I didn't want a rebound girlfriend.

One night we went to go see *Tatie Danielle*, a French film, and then we wound up back at her tiny apartment, where we talked till two o'clock in the morning. That was when it clicked. That night. No question. From then on we were a couple.

Leah brings out the best in me. In my first marriage, I became this spineless little turd. I'd roll over and do whatever I was told, all the time agreeing to things against my better judgment. Not so with Leah. She makes me feel good and smart—even though I'm not always smart. She makes me feel witty—even when

I'm not particularly witty. She loves me, not in spite of my idiosyncrasies, but because of them. I never have to apologize around her for being me.

And she makes me laugh. And she has a great smile.

## ON BENDED KNEE

### A run to the mall

We decided to move in together. I told her it was with the idea that we'd get married someday, but I swore to myself that that day would be at least a year off. During that year, she'd occasionally come home, punch me on the chest, and say, "Where's my ring? Where's my ring? Where's my ring?" But I waited a year. We were at this restaurant called Mirabelle. I waited till she went to the restroom, and I put the ring out on the table. She came out but didn't see it, so I had to point it out to her. She got all blushy and weepy. Of course, the ring didn't fit, so we wolfed down our dinners and ran to the mall to have it sized.

# T.G.

### *Never a second thought*

> *"I decided to marry her five minutes after meeting her," he says of Susan, to whom he*

*has been married since 1976. T.G. is in his
midforties and works as a traffic engineer. He
and Susan have two children.*

We'd been going together for about three months. I
was pretty intense and made no bones about the fact
that I was planning to marry her. Not hoping—planning. And I told her that on our first date.

Sometime in March 1976, she told me she wanted
to think things over, that we were seeing too much of
each other, that whole bit. I think I'd scared the wad-
ding out of her. I was pretty crazy. I gave her a kiss,
reminded her what my phone number was, and
walked. There was no fight, no harsh words, nothing
unpleasant at all. I simply told her when she was ready
to get married to give me a call.

After about a week, she called. That call was
understood by both of us as a tacit acceptance of my
marriage proposal. We never discussed it after that,
other than something that was going to happen. There
was only the question of when.

About ten months later, in my parents' kitchen (my
parents were in the room with us), that's when she
formally said yes and I gave her the engagement ring.
At the time, Susan and I were living with my parents,
it being the summer and the two of us not in school. My
mother gave us her engagement ring. Susan and I were
married five months later.

What did I find so attractive about her? Her love of life, her enthusiasm, her intelligence, our common values on a number of things, our respected differences. What's not attractive? Not one damned thing that I can think of. My relationship, my marriage to Susan, is *my life*.

## FIRST GLANCE

### Getting out the vote

The first time I saw her, we were both working the student elections at the University of Oregon. She had been assigned to one voting station and her partner had not shown up, so I was sent out from the elections board to fill in. She was sitting down behind a table in front of the Erb Memorial Union gift shop, wearing a red turtleneck sweater. She was damn good-looking and animated and had interesting things to say in response to some of my more off-the-wall comments about passersby. I knew for certain that I'd just met my future wife.

# David D.
*Beating the odds*

> *A TV news producer in his late twenties,*
> *David began courting colleague Nancy as she*

*was coming off of a nasty divorce. "She wasn't*
*looking for another companion so soon, I was*
*eight years younger than her, and my last*
*name was very similar to her ex-husband's*
*last name," says David. "Add it all up, and I*
*didn't have a prayer. But I hung in there." This*
*conversation took place two weeks before his*
*and Nancy's wedding.*

We'd been getting to be close friends, and I'd been trying to get her to go out with me for six months, but she
insisted she wasn't interested in dating. Then one day
we were hanging out at my apartment, sitting on the
couch laughing about something. I knew if we stayed
there, I'd try to kiss her and she'd hate me and it'd
ruin our friendship. So I moved away and explained
why I was moving away. She said she had to leave,
and I walked her to her car. But before she got in, she
leaned over and kissed me. Five minutes later, we dis-
engaged. Wow.

A few days later, we went out on our first real date,
dinner at a nice restaurant and a show by Billy Con-
nolly, a Scottish comedian. We had a wonderful time,
the conversation was real easy, and the kissing in the
car afterward, as the rain came down and the windows
fogged up, is something I'll never forget. We dated for
the next four years or so and then decided to marry.

I had been ready—perhaps more than ready—for marriage at that point. I'm happiest when I have companionship, and I've always wanted kids. Until I met Nancy, though, I didn't think I'd ever find a woman I'd want to spend the rest of my life with who would also want to spend her life with me. I guess I was kind of adhering to that old Groucho Marx line, about not wanting to join any club that would have me as a member.

All I knew about Nancy was that I was happiest when we were together, and everything suffered when we were fighting or apart. I wanted this woman in my life, my whole life, every day of my life. And despite my feelings it would never happen, she, it turned out, wanted the same of me.

What was it about her that made her so attractive to me? She's pretty and fun to be with. But the main thing about Nancy is how she thinks and feels about things. It's her marvelous, beautiful, caring, elaborate soul. The more I find out about her, the more I want to know.

## ON BENDED KNEE

### An ocean, a flower, a dog

Nancy and I love the ocean. When she suggested that we drive down to the Florida panhandle for a few days, I saw my chance. it was right before sunset when we arrived. Perfect. We checked into our bed-and-breakfast and walked to the beach. When we got there, I told her I had sketched her a tulip (her favorite flower, and my nickname for her). I added that I had shown my sketch to "a friend," and he came up with *this*—and, dropping to one knee, I pulled out a diamond engagement ring in the shape of an abstract tulip, which I'd had a jeweler design. At that very moment, a large, friendly dog came bounding up. He landed one paw on my bent knee and the other on Nancy's arm. An older lady came puffing up apologetically. "He just wants to be in on the excitement," she said. To which Nancy replied, "You don't know the half of it—my boyfriend just proposed!" The woman, looking amazed, hugged us both, wished us well, and pulled the dog away. I made some crack about having been blessed by the beasts, and Nancy eventually remembered to say yes to my proposal.

## Tony D.
*Muscular love*

> He is a former national bodybuilding champion
> and owner and manager of an exercise-equipment

*store. In 1994, at age thirty-nine, he married*
*for the first time.*

When I met Kathy I was in the process of leaving the girlfriend I'd lived with, on and off, for seven years, so I wasn't really looking to jump into anything too fast.

We had our first date about three weeks after we met. We went to a bodybuilding competition. I was a judge. It was fantastic. We both had a great time. Kathy was the sweetest girl I'd ever met. Very laid-back. Very understanding. Didn't drink. Didn't smoke. I know that sounds boring. But, believe me, it's just what the doctor ordered. I can be kind of a crazy guy. I need someone like her in my life.

I fell in love with her, just like I've been falling in love with every girl I've dated ever since I was fourteen. I always magnify their good qualities. That's how I am. Kathy and I decided to move in together, and that's when we first talked marriage. With her strict Catholic upbringing, we felt it would be best to get engaged. She wanted a big church wedding. I would have gladly settled for a backyard barbecue. But Kathy got her way. And even though her father popped some bills for the reception, we were still in the hole ten Gs.

Reservations about getting married? I guess I had one big one—I wasn't sure if I'd be bored sexually with the same girl. In a sense my fears were justified. I don't know if the same kind of intenseness could ever be there, like it once was. Part of that is the loss of novelty. But things also change over the years for a guy. I'm not complaining, though. There's more to marriage than just sex. It's real nice to come home at the end of the day to somebody who is excited to see me and lets me know that I've been missed.

I think what really makes a marriage work is having things to share and compatible lifestyles. Kathy and I are both totally dedicated to fitness, and that carries over to what we eat, the vitamins we take, and the things we do, like going to [bodybuilding] competitions.

## FIRST GLANCE

### Doing squats

I met Kathy at the health club I was managing. It was my first day, and she was doing a leg workout. I stopped over to introduce myself and made a suggestion as to how she could do better squats. I'm a firm believer in doing squats to work the front of the thighs. She was receptive to my suggestions. I took a good look at her, and I saw a very attractive girl, with nice eyes, who appeared to be committed to her physique. She reminded me of Gabriela Sabatini, the tennis champ.

# Hal
## *Young and hopeful*

> *He is twenty-one and about to enter his senior*
> *year of college, where he majors in psychology*
> *and edits the school paper. He and Stephanie*
> *met when he was nineteen. He plans to marry*
> *her. "When she is ready," he says.*

She had just transferred into my high school and was
living only two blocks away. I'd seen her around, at the
bus stop and in the hallways, and thought she was real
cute. But I was nervous about approaching her. One
day we were on the public bus together. She was sitting two seats behind me. All of a sudden she says to
me, "How do I get off the bus?" I turned to her, and she
was looking all flushed and embarrassed. It turns out
that was her first time ever on a public bus, and she
didn't know about pulling the cord. I was really happy
that she spoke to me.

On our first date, we went to go see a movie, *The
Good Son*, and then we went to Baskin Robbins to get
some ice cream. We were sitting out on the patio, and
she told me how the average person unwittingly con-
sumes eight spiders a year. Wow, I thought, what a
girl! That night, on the side of her garage, we kissed
for the first time. It was incredible, a long kiss, after

which we stood for a few seconds and just looked at each other.

Stephanie's from California, where people are really outgoing. In Pennsylvania, people aren't, so she was having a tough time making friends. We started spending all our time together. By graduation, I was thinking very seriously about marriage. I had enormous amounts of fun doing things with her—even doing *nothing* with her, just sitting around on the grass. We'd do that for hours. And every time I was without her, like cleaning my room or hanging out, I'd wish she were there.

Lately, we've gone through some ups and downs. We were originally planning to get married her junior year of college. (Stephanie is two years behind me.) Now we're just getting over a rough period, and she says she's unsure. Me, I think getting engaged at this point would help us get over a lot of our problems, which are rooted in jealousy. I'm certain I want to get married—but only at a pace that she's comfortable with. I'd rather do it right than do it rushed.

## REFLECTIONS

**No need to sow**

I know I'm not typical for a guy my age. I can't wait to get married, settle down, and be with one

woman for the rest of my life. Most other guys want
to sow their wild oats. I can understand that. I'm just
different.

# Ben
## *He found his damsel*

> *He met Ann in October 1994, in America
> Online's Tattoos & Piercing Chat Room. "I had
> a few tattoos, she had a few—that was our
> first common interest," he says. Ben is twenty-
> seven, a computer technician with an interest
> (which he shares with Ann) in medieval
> history and mythology. (His tattoos include a
> castle, a wizard, and a unicorn.) He and Ann
> married a year after connecting on-line, seven
> months after meeting face-to-face. At the time
> of this interview, Ann was seven months
> pregnant with their first child.*

I knew I wanted to get married someday, but when I first
met Ann I can't say I was looking for a long-term relationship. I don't think she was either. We just seemed to
have a lot in common, which is why that first night we
met on-line we chatted till morning. Then I called her on
the phone a week later (I was in South Carolina, she was

in Pennsylvania), and we spoke for eight hours. My phone bill at the end of the month was $500!

A few more marathon phone calls over the next three months, and I decided to come up and see her. Sure, I wanted to meet her face-to-face. But it was also this great adventure for me. I had never been out of South Carolina, and I wanted to see other places. Ann gave me an excuse.

I first saw her at the front door of her house. (She was living with her parents.) She was awfully nervous, had a hard time speaking, and the conversation didn't go anywhere. She was washing dishes, cleaning the floor, anything to keep from making eye contact with me. I was plenty nervous, too, but I've always been shy and probably wouldn't have had much to say anyway.

Eventually things eased up and we started talking, and it didn't take long before we were a couple. I wound up staying a week, and then she came back to South Carolina with me for another ten days. Four months later, I resigned from my job and moved north to be with her. Six months later, we started talking marriage.

For me, getting married was about security, having someone to always be there, to be supportive financially and emotionally. I also wanted to have the image of being married. I wanted for people (including prospective employers) to look at me and say, "Oh, Ben. He's married. He's someone who knows how to commit." Having kids was important, too. I'd like three. Having children, raising them, educating them . . . that's what life is all about.

Why Ann? She's smart. She's honest. I know she won't cheat on me or give away my secrets. Those are the most important things. I don't think you can look for perfection in a partner. You've got to pick up with someone whose flaws you can live with. I can live with hers. She can live with mine.

## A WEDDING TALE

### Creative anachronism

Our wedding had a medieval theme—women in long gowns, men in tunics with musketeer hats. We had been legally married in the courthouse the day before. The wedding itself was just a big party and show. Ann's brother did the ceremony dressed in medieval garb. We did the stepping over the sword. Ann made most of the costumes, and we prepared much of the food. The whole thing only cost us $1,500. We weren't going into hock so that we could have an expensive reception. That's one tradition I think is better left in the past!

# Yves

*Classroom pursuit*

> *He met Virginie in college in 1983. They were*
> *married three years later. Yves, who was born*
> *and lives in Strasbourg, France, is thirty-two*
> *years old. He works as a product and systems*
> *manager for a large bank, practices judo, and*
> *runs distance races.*

So much of our relationship was based on chance—or
fate. We met in the classroom. She was wearing all
black, sitting to my side. I leaned over, asked her name,
and touched her lightly on the knee. I swear, it was
nothing but a friendly gesture! But that was the last
time that she sat next to me!

Months rolled by, years, and we kept winding up
in the same classes. Although she'd sit a seat or two
away, she was still friendly. She was also a much better student than I was. (I was more into sports than
studying.) I started to borrow her course materials
and class notes, which she was fairly gracious about,
considering.

After graduation, I applied to several schools to do
postgraduate work. The only school I got accepted to
was the business school in Nancy. On the first day of
class, I wasn't really expecting to know anybody, but

who do I see? Virginie. The classrooms were much smaller than in our undergrad years. She couldn't get too far from me!

Over time, we became buddies. One night I was at her place, and there I was sitting close by her side. At one point, I looked at her and felt the urge to embrace her. I said to myself, "If you take her in your arms, you'll marry her." I leaned over and gave her a hug. That was it. After that moment, there was *no* doubt in my mind: we were going to be husband and wife.

She is everything I could want in a wife . . . Sweet, calm, down-to-earth, friendly, and intelligent (intelligence is very important). She's neither possessive nor jealous. She has a truly warm spirit—although, boy, she can get hot tempered at times! Above all, most of the time when I'm with her, I feel good about myself; I feel at peace.

In January 1990, we told her parents we were engaged. In August, we had our civil wedding. In June, we were wed in the church. In my mind, getting married is a way that a man forms his station in society and allows for children, which give him a certain degree of immortality. Our two daughters, Camille and Pauline, were born on February 12, 1992.

# CONCLUSION

## So Why Do Men Marry?

To sum up why men get hitched, I'll suggest the four most common answers I got from the men I surveyed, the chapter titles to Part Two of this book—pleasure, pragmatism, procreation, and purpose. But, still, such things can certainly be had without the throwing of rice and the exchanging of vows. So I must suggest two additional explanations . . .

# ADDITIONAL EXPLANATION 1
## Who the hell knows?

Why do men marry? Why do suburbanites kill pretty little dandelions? Why do we say "bless you" when someone sneezes? Why does the waitress refill your coffee for free but charge you for an extra cup of tea? These are all cultural institutions, and institutions often just *are*. You can't analyze them nor find logical explanations for them. Such may be the case for why men marry.

The same applies if you think of men's drive to marry as instinctual, as some do. Asking why men follow their instincts and pair off with a woman is like asking a duck why it quacks or a dog why it chases cats and squirrels. Don't hold your breath waiting for a logical explanation.

# ADDITIONAL EXPLANATION 2
## Why in the world not?

On the other hand, marriage is an awfully good deal for men. As such, there's nothing more logical than marriage. Surveys show that married men are happier.

They get more-frequent promotions at work. Married male politicians are more likely to get elected. Married men have a 23 percent lower risk of heart attack and a life expectancy of ten years beyond the bachelor. Surveys show they have twice as much sex as single guys. And they are much more likely to walk out the door in the morning with matching pants and socks.

And doesn't everyone want matching pants and socks?

## About the Author

Russell Wild was born in New York City on December 25, 1955. He has worked at various times as a credit analyst in a bank, an advertising salesman, an environmental activist, a yoga instructor, and a senior editor at a large publishing house. He writes regularly for national magazines and is the author of several books, including *Games Bosses Play* (Contemporary, 1997) and *Business Briefs* (Peterson's/Pacesetter, 1996). In addition to writing, Wild is also a professional speaker and personal performance coach. He lives in Allentown, Pennsylvania, with his wife, Susan, an attorney, and their two children, Addie and Clay. He can be reached at Rwild@Compuserve.com.